GRANDPARENTING

Creating & Keeping a Lasting Legacy

Roger & Dottie Small

WITH KAREN DAVIS

MORNING JOY MEDIA
Spring City, Pennsylvania

Published by Morning Joy Media. Visit www.morningjoymedia.com for more information on bulk discounts and special promotions, or e-mail your questions to info@morningjoymedia.com.

Design: Debbie Capeci
Front cover photo—great-grandson Josiah, grandson Matthew, son-in-law Michael, & Roger: Brian Baker
Back cover photo—Roger & great-granddaughter Lucy: "Generations of Love" by Julie Moon
Photo of authors in back matter: Kristie Michelle Photography

Subject Headings:

1. Christian life. 2. Grandparenting—Religious aspects—Christianity.

ISBN 978-1-937107-63-5 (pbk)
ISBN 978-1-937107-64-2 (ebook)

Printed in the United States of America

NOTE: Names of individuals in authors' stories (other than family members) have been changed for privacy.

DEDICATION

We dedicate this book...

To our heavenly Father, because of His grace and mercy;

To Jesus Christ, our Savior and Lord;

To the Holy Spirit, for His enabling power and inspiration to write this book;

> *Unless the LORD builds the house, they labor in vain who build it* (Psalm 127:1).

To our three daughters, Kim, Robin, and Lisa, and their husbands, who have blessed us with our thirteen grandchildren and sixteen great-grandchildren—and counting!

> *For the Lord is good; His mercy is everlasting, and His truth endures to all generations* (Psalm 100:5).

CONTENTS

FOREWORD

One generation shall commend your works to another, and shall declare your mighty acts.... They shall speak of the might of your awesome deeds, and I will declare your greatness. They shall pour forth the fame of your abundant goodness and shall sing aloud of your righteousness (Psalm 145:4, 6–7 ESV).

This wonderful charge is given to those who know Jesus Christ as their Savior, to tell the next generation about His greatness and grace. I have had the privilege of knowing Roger and Dottie Small for more than forty-two years, the last thirty-six years as their son-in-law. They are fulfilling this Great Commission. I am personally experiencing the wonderful fruit of their parenting by enjoying marriage with their oldest daughter, Kim (the most godly and beautiful woman I can imagine), and have seen them up close and personal as grandparents to our children. Not only have they excelled as parents to their three daughters, as in-laws to their three sons, but they have also been excellent grandparents to all thirteen of their grandchildren as well as their sixteen great-grandchildren. Their lives "sing aloud" of the goodness and faithfulness of God to our family.

This is a couple that has lived to serve the next generation. They have done that with their time, energy, and resources. They have consistently postured themselves to support us because, in their own words, "It is our children's time now; our children are the ones doing the 'more important work.'" Roger and Dottie have been selfless in the ways they are living out this season of their lives. Rather than come across as "experts," they have specifically encouraged us in our parenting as well as in our marriages. Because of the testimony of their genuine humility, we (the next generation) only *want* to relate to them and learn from them more and more. Their godly character, love for the Savior and the church, and their desire to put our interests above their own have modeled for all to see Christ's heart to serve. They have left their children, grandchildren, and great-grandchildren a wonderful Christian legacy and powerful example to follow.

You have in your hands some of the fruit of their labors. I am excited that they have revised their first book and believe this book will go even further in encouraging and equipping its readers to serve the next generation and show them the great worth of our Savior. While you may not be able to imitate all they have done, with the same help of God's grace that they have experienced, you can certainly imitate their hearts.

Mom and Dad, on behalf of your girls, your sons-in-law, your grandchildren, and your great-grandchildren, *thank you* for your example and for modeling Christ-exalting godliness to multiple generations. We love you!

—WARREN BOETTCHER
SENIOR PASTOR, SOVEREIGN GRACE CHURCH

INTRODUCTION

Incline your ears to the words of my mouth. . . .
Which we have heard and known,
And our fathers have told us.
We will not hide them from their children,
Telling to the generation to come the praises of the LORD,
And His strength and His wonderful works that He has done. . . .
Which He commanded our fathers,
That they should make them known to their children;
That the generation to come might know them,
The children who would be born,
That they may arise and declare them to their children,
That they may set their hope in God,
And not forget the works of God,
But keep His commandments.

—Psalm 78:1–7

Grandparents. Say the word to young people today, and one garners a wide array of responses: *Wise. Experienced. Huggable. Slow. Permissive. Indulgent. Patient. Out of touch. Close. Distant.*

Whatever personal adjectives one uses to describe us, we do have a significant role to play! God has set us in extended families, specifically and intentionally. It is by *His* design that families are a blend of both young and old.

Recently, Dottie and I were reflecting on our place in our growing family as we watched a little family of sparrows nest just outside our kitchen window. It wasn't long before the tiny eggs hatched, and soon miniature chirping heads peered above the rim of the nest. Although Ma and Pa Sparrow were doting and attentive to their new brood, they nudged the fledgling birds out of the nest surprisingly early. A mere ten days later, under the watchful eyes of two parents, the young siblings perched precariously on the edge of the nest, then glided to the ground, their immature wings unaccustomed to flight. Their first steps away from the security of home were tentative and weak, rendering them earthbound at first. Quite suddenly, two generations of sparrows spread their wings in unison and took flight, each ascending in a different direction, independent of one another, not looking back.

God's design for families is a model that we simply cannot afford to lose.

We were captivated as we reflected on the contrast between human relationships and those of sparrows. How uniquely God has designed our families to be relational and nurturing. We are the crown of God's creation. He sets us in families for a lifetime, making a place for each member of the extended family. He intentionally includes us older folks in the nest! God affirms the aged, as in the book of Job: *"Wisdom is with aged men, and with length of days, understanding"* (Job 12:12).

At the same time, we are aware of how easily we can become like the independent sparrows, if we do not teach our young ones to value the precious gift of family that the Lord has given us. God's design for families is a model that we simply cannot afford to lose.

In many ways, families have strayed from the benevolent design of our heavenly Father. We live in an age when courts, lawmakers, and social reformers presume to redefine what makes up a family. But the reality is that the structure of a family was God's design in the first place. After God created Adam, he declared that it was not good for man to be alone. So, God created a companion for Adam, a helpmate—a *woman*—taken from man's side. Children were added to Adam and Eve, husband and wife, as a blessing upon what God had already created as *good*.

With an agenda to destroy what the Lord has declared good, Satan has been out to destroy families ever since Adam's fall in the garden of Eden. God's love for families, however, could not be thwarted. God was determined to pour out His covenant blessings upon families—a covenant that would cost Him His own beloved Son.

This book is our family's story. But God is simply using our family to write His story. We are an ordinary family passing down the legacy of an extraordinary God. This is the story of our joys and successes as grandparents; it is also the story of our failures—and what we have learned from them. It's the story of God's plan for multigenerational families. Many have encouraged us to write this book as a compilation of our experiences as a family of four generations, three of whom are presently living under one roof!

Our family embodies a paradigm that has been nearly lost in postmodern America. It is a model of multigenerational families living together, growing together, serving one another, making blunders together, and learning from one another. It's a model in which young people have the opportunity to glean wisdom from their elders, and we elders have the corresponding privilege of learning from our young people.

Whereas close-knit, multigenerational families were once the norm, they are no longer. Once upon a time, daughters customarily lived at home, under a father's covering of protection, until marriage. Today, that family arrangement is nearly nonexistent. On the contrary, we are prone to pass a critical eye upon grown children who still live with their parents, no matter what the reason.

We recognize that family situations are diverse and complex. Careers, distance, and illness are just a few factors that may disrupt the potential blessing of the close involvement of multigenerational family members in one another's lives. The web of separation grows even more tangled with the prevalence of out-of-wedlock babies, divorce, and the alienation of families that inevitably ensues. While the circumstances that prompt distancing from older generations may indeed be legitimate and validated in today's society, the end result can nonetheless be an emotional estrangement that accompanies a physical separation. Whatever the reason, we know many grandparents whose hearts are left hungry for closer involvement with their grandchildren.

God's model for families draws us back to His design—and the blessings that accompany it.

God's model for families draws us back to *His* design—and the blessings that accompany it. Families are God's idea, God's design, and God's ordained means to purify and sanctify individual members.

As the Lord's mouthpieces, it is our duty to proclaim His ways to the next generation if they are to experience His utmost blessings in the days to come! God's heart and will are to bless His people, and His blessings will be manifest, in part, in the restoration and strengthening of multigenerational family relationships. Widespread acceptance of these ideas would be radical in our times. They are the antithesis of the influence of our culture and the messages that many accept and embrace as normal. Yet we *cannot* lose the wisdom of the ancients that has been passed down through the millennia. To lose that would be to lose God in history.

We believe that the Lord wants to restore the foundation of strong families for His own glory! His design has been for families to care for one another across the generations—to learn from one another—to be knit together and to be sanctified together. Along with the obvious challenges, the joys and blessings of transgenerational families "doing life" together are becoming lost, in many cases.

While we are not advocating that children should always settle in close proximity to their parents, we are proposing that it would be a great loss if the *vision* for close, meaningful, interactive, multigenerational families were to be lost. With modern communication technology at our fingertips, this vision can still be preserved, even across geographic miles. We, too, face the challenge of having children and grandchildren living many miles away. Granted, long-distance relationships take more

We cannot deny that our role as grandparents often stretches us beyond our personal comfort zones.

forethought and creativity, but they can be every bit as close in heart and meaningful as with grandchildren who live nearby.

In today's culture, parenting is an exceptionally challenging job for young couples. What a blessing it can be for them when grandparents—whether living nearby or far away—are involved in their lives and their children's. We cannot deny that our role as grandparents often stretches us beyond our personal comfort zones. Our personal experience attests that we are certainly not growing any younger! Yet we can also testify heartily that building relationships with grandchildren can be a genuine gift from heaven, all the way around.

This book is our encouragement to grandparents to embrace their unique and significant role in the lives of their families. The special relationship between a grandparent and a grandchild is entirely different from the bond that exists between a parent and a child. Grandparenting, in comparison to the role of parenting, is a *grand* time of life!

As grandparents, we can bring a deep sense of stability and security to the home. It is meaningful for grandchildren to know that they are loved and accepted by others in addition to their parents. When we profess a faith that is real and personal, our influence on young lives is even more powerful. The perceptive little eyes of our grandchildren are watching closely and taking in everything about us. Our living testimony of faith can leave a profound imprint on their minds and hearts.

Dottie and I do not claim to have all the answers for successful grandparenting. There are too many complex life situations. But the Lord *does* have all the answers—and so, we direct you to Him. His grace is more than sufficient to enable you to grandparent in a way that honors Him. While your grandparenting may look different than ours, the biblical principles and God's favor are the same. It is our desire to bring hope, encouragement, and vision to you as grandparents.

You may play a more vital role in God's greater plan than what is presently visible to you.

We have a strong confidence that the Lord is raising up leaders among the next generation. But these forthcoming leaders will need lights to guide them and unshakable roots to anchor them in solid ground. Who will be the ones to provide light to guide them, and who will help to water their roots and prune their branches? It is we who are called to the task. *This* is the legacy we will leave to this upcoming generation.

Despite the many forces tugging families apart today, we believe the Lord is actively engaged in the business of restoring families. God's children are called to be lights to the world—we cannot permit his light to be extinguished. As believers in the Son of God, we have the privilege of relaying a bright torch to our heirs and playing a key role in the restoration of families.

If you are one of those who has experienced brokenness in your family, our hearts go out to you. Please do not put this book down yet! Grandparents are needed now more than ever. Even if man has marred God's desired plan for families, the answer is not to discard God's plan! His remedy is to restore what has been lost and to redeem it for His glory. Do not despair. It *can* happen in *your* family and in *your* situation. There is no one who is beyond the healing, restoring reach of a loving God! You may play a more vital role in God's greater plan than what is presently visible to you.

So what is this book all about? It's about two ordinary grandparents sharing their lives, their joys, and their failures. It's about seizing opportunities to sow seeds into the lives and hearts of our grandchildren—seeds that will bear fruit, both in this life and in the eternal life to come. It's about creating a family identity that our children, our grandchildren, and our great-grandchildren will be jealous to own and faithful to carry on.

So what is this book all about? It's about... seizing opportunities to sow seeds into the lives and hearts of our grandchildren—seeds that will bear fruit, both in this life and in the eternal life to come.

> *But as for me and my house, we will serve the LORD. . . . The LORD our God we will serve, and His voice we will obey!* (Joshua 24:14, 24).

Finally, this book is about leaving footprints of faith to guide those who follow after us: not only our grandchildren, but also the generations that follow them. Our footprints will guide them to rewards both seen and unseen.

While we do not look at the things which are seen, but at the things which are not seen. For the things which are seen are temporary, but the things which are not seen are eternal (2 Corinthians 4:18).

This book is filled with both theoretical insights and practical, real-life illustrations. It is our hope that God will use this to rekindle a vision that has nearly been lost in our generation—a vision for strong, faith-filled, multi-generational families unified in fellowship. The legacy of this vision will surely affect many generations to come. May this book you are holding be only the beginning, and may you delight in the journey along the way!

OUR PRAYER

Heavenly Father,

What the enemy is seeking to destroy, may You use for our good. May You redeem our families, strengthen our relationships, and restore Your godly design to families. May You draw the hearts of our children and grandchildren to the wisdom and love of those who have gone before them, and may You raise up generations who seek first Your kingdom and Your righteousness.

We ask You these things in the eternal name of Jesus Christ.

Amen.

1 • DOES OUR LEGACY MATTER?

Blessed is the man who fears the LORD,
Who delights greatly in His commandments.
His descendants will be mighty on Earth;
The generation of the upright will be blessed.
—Psalm 112:1–2

I t had been a hectic, sultry day in July as I sank into bed, anxious for a night of refreshing sleep. As on any other night, I fell asleep next to my husband, Roger, cozy and secure by his side. Little did either of us know that before the sun rose, something would happen that would change our whole world.

Suddenly, the phone crackled through the stillness, jarring me from my dreams. *Who on earth could be calling in the wee hours of the morning?* Apprehension roused me from my sleepy stupor as our bedside phone continued to ring in urgency. I fumbled to answer it.

"Hello? Hello? Who is this?" I persisted, *"Who is this?"*

"Mom! Mom! It's me, Warren!" Our son-in-law blurted into the phone.

"What's the matter? Is everything all right?"

"It's a *girl!*" Warren exclaimed.

"It's a girl? It's a girl?" I repeated groggily, trying to take in the enormity of the moment.

Now fully awake, it began to dawn on me that this was the phone call we had been anxiously awaiting. Our oldest daughter, Kimberly, had been expecting our first grandchild any day. My husband, only half-conscious, climbed from the covers and headed robotically in the direction of the bathroom. Holding my hand over the phone, I called after him, "Honey, it's a girl! We're *grandparents!*"

Roger halted mid stride and did an about-face. "Did I hear you say *we are grandparents?!*"

"Yes, honey. It's a *girl*. Our Kimberly is a mommy." Waves of emotion flooded through me.

Left dangling on the other end of the call, Warren prompted, "Mom, are you still there?"

"Yes! Yes! I'm just telling Dad about our new baby." Then I added anxiously,

"How is Kimberly?"

"She's exhausted. Her labor lasted for hours, but she's doing well."

"Oh, Warren, I'm so thankful for that. We'll be there as soon as we can pull ourselves together."

Just like that, we were grandparents. Uncharted territory. And we were unprepared. Now what do we do?

Hanging up the phone, giddy with joy and adrenaline, I realized that, in my enthusiasm, I forgot to ask our granddaughter's name. I tried in vain to call Warren back, but couldn't reach him. Roger and I dressed hastily, grabbed two bagels, and drove the twenty miles to the hospital in record time.

Glowing with the pride of a new father, Warren met us in the hallway and escorted us in to see Kim. She looked radiant yet exhausted at the same time. Warren, holding her hand affectionately, commended her, "I'm so proud of Kimberly. She did so well. But now she needs to rest. I'll take you down to see Julie Dawn." *Julie Dawn*. So *that* was our granddaughter's name!

Warren strode purposefully ahead of us, much faster than we could follow. Either he was anxious to see his new baby, or we were slowing down with age. Surely it wasn't the latter!

Standing in front of the nursery, Warren pointed proudly to our first grandchild—as if we needed help to recognize the family resemblance.

"Look, Mom and Dad! There she is—the beautiful one right over there!"

Enfolded in a soft pink blanket with a pink cap hugging her head, our precious baby granddaughter was carried by the nurse closer to the window so we could scrutinize her in more detail. Carefully, the nurse unwrapped her a bit so we could count all her fingers and toes.

"That's my daughter. Isn't she beautiful?" her proud daddy murmured in a tone I had never heard him use before.

"Oh my. You're so right. She *is* beautiful," we ardently agreed, as we all attempted to grasp the wonder of this miraculous moment.

The sight of Julie's little rosebud mouth suddenly transported my thoughts back to the day twenty-three years ago when Kimberly, my own first baby, was placed in my arms, and I savored the sweetness of the memory and this moment.

At seven pounds, two ounces and nineteen inches long, Julie Dawn made her debut, thus launching the next generation of our extended family. We grandparents—as well as all the aunts and uncles—could scarcely wait to embrace and enjoy this precious miracle from God.

Just like that, we were grandparents. Uncharted territory. And we were unprepared. *Now what do we do?*

After the seemingly never-ending years of diapers, disciplining, teaching, counseling, handing over car keys, and planning weddings for three daughters, suddenly Roger and I were thrust into a new and unfamiliar role as grandparents. In a quandary over our competency, we wondered, *Are we ready to step into this new role and fill the shoes of grandparents?*

Before baby Julie's arrival, we had entertained temptations to indulge ourselves in pleasures we had forgone while raising our family—buying a new car to replace our 1960 Ford station wagon, traveling abroad, building a new home, even taking a cruise. Although there was nothing inherently wrong with those desires, introducing a grandbaby into the family picture suddenly rearranged our priorities. She could not have known how much she would change our world, but little Julie Dawn had captivated our hearts. We were now hopelessly consumed with a desire to be an integral, significant part of her life—as well as the lives of future grandchildren with whom the Lord would bless us.

> **Introducing a grandbaby into the family picture suddenly rearranged our priorities.**

A new world was opening before us. As young and inexperienced grandparents, we could not help but wonder, *Where do we begin? How do we nurture a meaningful and personal relationship with a grandchild?*

Roger's and my experiences with our own grandparents provided not only insights, but also motivation to do this grandparenting thing well. Roger's maternal grandparents had never been involved in his life. For some unknown reason, his mother had not wanted her children to be involved with her parents. As a result, Roger did not receive as much as a birthday card or gift from his maternal grandparents.

Interaction with the paternal side of Roger's family was equally lacking; Roger's paternal grandparents were an older couple who were not interested in children. Thus, when young Roger observed his friends with their grandparents, he felt a wistful longing for the family connection they apparently enjoyed. Consequently, although Roger commenced his own journey into grandparenting without role models to emulate, he felt a strong desire to give our grandchildren the attention and love he himself had missed.

My family experience was quite different from my husband's. My father's parents lived near us on a farm, and that was the site of plentiful, warm childhood memories for me. I adored my dad's mother. My older brother, David, called her "Ginnah" because that's the way "Grandma" sounded to his two-year-old ears—and the name stuck. Ginnah was a kind woman. She was generous with both her time and her home-baked cookies. I loved being with her. Whenever my mom went shopping, she would drop me off at Ginnah's, much to my stomach's delight. Fresh-baked molasses cookies always filled a tin on the third shelf of Ginnah's pantry. My mouth still waters thinking about them! I also knew exactly where to find the crayons, coloring books, and story books in her den closet. She would lovingly read my favorite story, *Ferdinand the Bull,* over and over again as I snuggled into her lap. At the age of four, I found Ginnah's lap a happy place to be. She was the favored grandparent in the eyes of her grandchildren.

In contrast to his wife, Ginnah's husband, my grandfather Robinson, was a rather stern man. He believed that "children were to be seen but not heard." Children's opinions did not matter, while adults were to be respected and obeyed.

On the other side of the family tree, my mother's parents lived far away in Boston, so we rarely saw them. However, when we did, the visits were memorable. Sometimes in the summers, Grandma and Grandpa Leavitt would babysit for a week while my parents vacationed. My grandmother Leavitt detested our house cat named Kelly. The cat annoyed her by weaving in between and around her legs while she was washing dishes. One morning when she was particularly provoked, she shouted, "If that cat doesn't stop bugging me, I am going to kick it into the middle of next week!" This so frightened me that I grabbed the cat and ran out of the house. For the rest of week, I made sure that Kelly kept her distance from Grandma!

My grandfather Leavitt was fussy with his tools. Everything had to be in its rightful place. One day my younger brother, four-year-old Doug, disturbed one of Grandpa's tools. When my grandfather wasn't looking, my older brother struck dread in little Doug's heart by telling him that Grandpa was going to spank him. Doug was so frightened that he scurried away and hid. No one could find him.

Finally, in desperation, my grandparents called the police. After three fruitless hours spent searching two hundred acres of farmland—including outbuildings, a pond, and an apple orchard—on a hunch, my older brother climbed up to the third floor of the barn to look around. This spot had been our favorite place to hide when we did not want to play with Doug, knowing he could never climb that high to find us. On this day, how Doug's little legs ever scampered up to the third floor remains a mystery. Perhaps fear had motivated him to defy his physical limitations, for the third floor of the barn is precisely where my older brother found the culprit. Little Doug was lying flat on his stomach, quivering in terror. The police carried a very frightened little boy down the ladder and reunited him with his fretting family. I remember that my grandfather had a few choice words to share with my older brother—who never pulled *that* again.

Like Roger, our own three daughters had unfortunately not experienced much grandparent involvement either. Roger's stepmother and father lived in Florida, and our girls only saw them when they drove north and south twice a year. Roger's father had a great sense of humor and loved to tell stories. I regret that our girls missed out on the benefit of a friendship with him.

Since my parents lived eight hours away in New England, it was difficult for them to build any kind of consistent relationship with our girls; nevertheless, they took advantage of every opportunity. On

Thanksgiving we eagerly packed our suitcases and drove to see my parents and grandparents. During the Christmas holidays, either they visited us, or we traveled to their New England farm.

I remember one Christmas when my father decided to create a memorable moment for our three daughters. Before we arrived at the farm, Dad had cut down a Christmas tree in the woods and left it stuck in a snow bank, looking as if it had grown there. I can still remember his twinkle as he anticipated the surprise it would be for the girls to find. I think my mother was behind this scheme in some way. She loved to be part of little creative games. When we arrived at the farm, my father and mother met us with great excitement. Christmas had officially begun.

I regret that our girls missed out on the benefit of a friendship with Roger's father.

Dad could not wait to propose his plan to the girls, "Hey, how about you girls come with me, and we'll cut down the Christmas tree together this year?"

"Really, Grandpa? Can we do that?"

"Yep, I know just the tree. But you better dress warmly. It's freezing out there."

I never saw the girls dress so fast. "We're ready, Grandpa!" they chimed eagerly.

My father put the three girls on a sled, and we trudged out to the woods. My mother, Roger, and I hung back to watch the adventure unfold.

"Look over there, girls. What do you think about that tree?" Dad had led them to the planted tree.

"That's the one," they all agreed.

My father commenced pretending to cut down the tree. Then he feigned needing help, asking the girls, "Will you help me? This tree is tough to pull out."

Three little pairs of mittens willingly gripped the trunk of the small pine tree, and with one yank, they pulled it up out of the snow. They were so proud of their accomplishment! I don't think they ever suspected my father's mischievous scheme.

We spent our summers with my Grandfather and Grandmother Leavitt in New Hampshire, at the small lakeside cabin they had built there in 1936. My parents had also built their own vacation home beside the cabin, creating a warm retreat that has been the site of many memories, transcending four generations.

No one can grandparent your grandchildren better than you.

When Roger and I were newly married, sharing time with my folks at the lake was a particularly special time for him. There, amid the love and laughter of my family, Roger's childhood longing for grandparents was fulfilled, as my family became his family.

Three generations later, as I gazed into the trusting eyes of our first grandchild and perceived the newfound joy in our son-in-law and daughter, I wondered, *What legacy would we pass on to this new generation?*

THOUGHTS TO PONDER

No one can grandparent your grandchildren better than *you*. While you may not do everything perfectly, God has made you the perfect grandparent for *your* grandchildren! God created your grandchildren to bring Himself glory, to bring you joy, and to be recipients of the legacy you leave them, which they will in turn pass down to their children. Your life does make a difference. You are still in the game, and you are needed. Even if you are separated by distance, with today's cell phones, Skype, and FaceTime, you can be wonderfully involved in the lives of your grandchildren—although you may need your grandchildren to teach you how to use these modern technologies! (That in itself has been a bonding experience for us!) These improved modes of electronic communication permit us to reach our little ones, whether they are near or far. Better means of communication enable extended families to stay connected so that grandparents can have an active role in shaping and inspiring the next generation.

OUR PRAYER

Dear heavenly Father,

We would like to be more involved in our grandchildren's lives, but we don't know how. Help us to find our place in this new role. We respect that these little ones are the responsibility of their parents, but we deeply care about them and their futures. Lord, help us to be more available and make us more aware of how we can bless our grandchildren.

As they grow older, may we develop special relationships with each of them. Let our love make a difference in the unfolding of their destinies.

May the gospel be lived and shared through this generation and all those who follow them, for Your glory. May our future grandchildren and great-grandchildren know You and love You—and may they surpass us in following You faithfully.

We love You, Jesus, and we pray this in Your name.

Amen.

2 • WHAT LEGACY WILL
WE LEAVE?

*Choose for yourselves this day whom you will serve, ... But as for
me and my house, we will serve the LORD.*

—Joshua 24:15

Rewind the clock thirty years, to the time Dottie and I first
began our own journey into the role of grandparenting. We
had so many unanswered questions swirling around in our
minds. *What could we glean from our own experiences with our grandparents? Had we missed any valuable lessons? What does it look like to create a lasting legacy for our children's children?* Finding answers to those
questions suddenly became of utmost importance to us. At that time,
we had no answers. We were treading blindly in uncharted territory.

There was one thing we did know with certainty: we wanted to be
actively involved in our grandchildren's lives. We longed to develop
comfortable, personal, trusting relationships with each of them. But
how could we do that when some of them lived miles away? Even with
the grandchildren who lived nearby, there were hurdles to overcome.
How could we participate in their lives without interfering in our
grown children's marriages and parenting preferences?

If the challenges of being new grandparents felt daunting to us, the
desire to leave a lasting and meaningful legacy was even more so. Until
we became grandparents, we had not given two thoughts to the matter

of creating a family legacy. We had to admit how little we knew about the subject and how misinformed some of our views were. At the time, we were inclined to buy into ways the world defines a legacy: "A legacy is about *us;* it's about our reputation. It is what we will be remembered for after we are gone."

Wanting to prepare ourselves for our exciting new role as grandparents, we turned to the Scriptures for guidance. We were hoping the timeless pages would reveal any meaningful influence we might have in the lives of our grandchildren.

The first thing we discovered was that a legacy is something passed down, or bequeathed, from one generation to the next. Whether it is material, like an inheritance, or nonmaterial, like a family reputation, a legacy is a thing of considerable worth. It is well worth safeguarding.

Wanting to prepare ourselves for our exciting new role as grandparents, we turned to the Scriptures for guidance.

Dottie and I began to see that a godly legacy is not about us at all; it is about something we *give to others.* What we give can be as simple, yet precious and enduring, as special memories, well-timed words of encouragement, and apt words of wisdom. A legacy is that which flows from within us, that which is visible to others.

The world can make a legacy feel like a burden when it is an unattainable standard to achieve: "What do I need to do that is good enough or important enough to qualify as a legacy?" In contrast to the world's arduous standard, a godly legacy is refreshingly simple. It is about living a life of simply trusting and obeying the Lord.

A vision for leaving a legacy to our grandchildren was coming into focus more clearly for us. Our thoughts drifted to one of the staples of our culture, sports legacies—athletes whom generations of boys and girls have aspired to emulate. If our culture has such fervor for athletic legacies, just imagine with us for a moment how incredible it would be if our grandchildren desired to emulate Jesus Christ! Oh, if only our grandsons and granddaughters could see Christ in us and thereby be drawn to our Savior Himself! We were beginning to envision the glorious and powerful impact a grandparent's legacy could have on the generations that follow us.

On the other end of the spectrum, we need to consider the consequences of leaving an adverse or detrimental legacy for future generations to follow. How much of an impact does an unfavorable legacy really have on future generations? Dottie and I were curious enough to begin searching through the Scriptures for answers. In doing so, we made some remarkable discoveries—fascinating accounts of tribes and patriarchs who left both positive and negative legacies for those who followed in their footsteps.

A HINT OF HISTORY

THE RECHABITES

Numbers 10:29; Judges 1:16; 1 Chronicles 2:55

The Rechabites were not Israelites. They were descendants of Abraham, though they were from his second wife, Keturah. Abraham and Keturah had a son named Midian, from whom was descended Jethro, the father-in-law of Moses. Although the Rechabites were not Israelites from the lineage of Abraham and Sarah, nevertheless, they probably held a belief in one God.

In Numbers 10:29, Moses invited Jethro, his father-in-law, to stay with the children of Israel. Jethro, a Rechabite, accepted the invitation, and his people settled as a separate tribe among the Israelites.

Descending from Jethro and the Rechabites was Jehonadab. Jehonadab was obedient to the Lord and helped to purge Israel of idol worship in the days of King Ahab. Jehonadab also, like his forefathers, instructed his family how to live righteously among the Jewish people. He commanded his sons and grandsons not to drink wine, build houses, plant fields, or grow vineyards. By not raising crops, the Rechabites' lifestyle did not interfere with the lives of the Jewish people among whom they lived. Instead, the Rechabites became nomads, lived in tents, and raised successive generations.

Jehonadab left to his descendants a godly legacy of obedience to the Lord. His family likewise had high respect for their father's wisdom. As a result, they not only lived in safety, health, and peace, but also in the Lord's favor for many generations. As Jehonadab had foreseen, the Rechabites were able to live peaceably in the land of the Israelites. The family legacy of abstinence from wine helped them to sustain the high moral character of the family. When the king of Babylon rose against their land, the Rechabites were granted refuge in Jerusalem, for the Lord was pleased with their obedience to their father's legacy and very disappointed with the disobedience of His own people (Jeremiah 35:16–17).

KING SAUL

Joshua 9:3–16; 2 Samuel 21:8–9

In bitter contrast to Jehonadab's legacy of obedience to the Lord is the account of King Saul. As king, Saul unjustly persecuted the Gibeonites, in violation of the covenant that Joshua had made with them.

When the Lord commanded Moses to give Joshua the Promised Land and to destroy all the inhabitants of the land, the inhabitants of nearby Gibeon feared for their lives. To preserve their lives, the Gibeonites deceived Joshua into believing they were sojourners from far away—not a neighboring tribe who needed to be destroyed. Consequently, Joshua swore an oath to the Gibeonites that he would let them live. As a result of Joshua's merciful legacy and faithfulness to uphold his oath, the Gibeonites lived peacefully among the Israelites and served them for many years, until the reign of King Saul.

When Saul came to the throne of Israel, he violated the treaty that Joshua had sworn to the Gibeonites. Because of this broken covenant, when David succeeded Saul as king, David avenged the Gibeonites. This resulted in the deaths of seven of Saul's sons—a heavy price for a father to pay for breaching an oath. Imagine the heartache and grief in that family. The tragic consequence of Saul's violation of a covenant was the calamity that was visited upon the next generation of his family.

MOSES

Judges 18

Although Moses is recognized as a righteous patriarch in the house of Israel, the infamous legacy of his descendants through his sons, Gershom and Elizer, was most surprising to us. Moses, known as the *Lawgiver,* walked with God and led Israel uprightly for many years. It was, therefore, unexpected when Jonathan, the son of Gershom and grandson of Moses, left his family, journeyed north, and became a pagan priest. Jonathan conducted religious services before idols for the family of Micah. It took only two generations for the progeny of the man who spoke with God face to face to become a pagan idolater.

To us, the outcome of the generations of Moses' offspring is heart-rending. As we reflected on the idolatrous fall of Moses' grandson, we had to wonder how it could have happened, considering the righteous legacy Moses had left him. Surely Jonathan knew that his grandfather had *walked and talked with God* and had *parted the Red Sea!* Furthermore, we found no biblical references to suggest that Moses' sons and grandsons were not instructed in the Law.

This unexpected outcome opened our eyes to the reality that, in only one generation, the gospel message of Jesus Christ could potentially be lost in our own family—if we were not conscientious to model godly living and faithful to share the gospel with our grandchildren. The Lord awakened in us a sober, reverent awe for the responsibility of godly grandparenting. *We could no longer be passive in our role as grandparents nor be content to live on the fringes of our grandchildren's lives!*

Having been sobered by the stories of biblical patriarchs like Jehonadab, Moses, and King Saul, we began to see more clearly that our new role as grandparents was a solemn responsibility that could affect generations to come. How grateful we were to know that the Lord's gentle hand would surely lead us through the uncharted waters of grandparenting and help us to understand and fulfill this role in the days and years ahead!

THOUGHTS TO PONDER

In spite of our shortsightedness, Dottie and I learned an important lesson about the role of grandparents. Although we meant well in our desire to see our grandchildren walking with the Lord, we mistakenly believed that we played a greater role in their salvations than we actually did. We needed to have our thinking overhauled. It was not our place to assume a false responsibility for their spiritual walks, as we learned from the life of Moses' grandson. While parents do bear responsibility to raise their children in the wisdom and admonition of the Lord and in the love of Jesus, it is the Spirit of God alone who leads children to salvation. *"For the grace of God has appeared that offers salvation to all people"* (Titus 2:11 NIV). When the Holy Spirit leads our grandchildren to the cross of salvation, it is each one's free choice whether to receive this gift. For us, the realization that salvation is one hundred percent in the hands of a loving and sovereign God lifted a needless burden from our shoulders and gave us the freedom to grandparent and pray in faith that the Lord would be in control of our grandchildren's lives.

For those who may be beginning their own journey into grandparenting, it may be disheartening or intimidating to confront the influences of our contemporary culture as it seeks to weaken and destroy families. Influences from all sides try to convince us that grandparents have no significant or useful place in the lives of our young people. But be encouraged! God Himself has given grandparents a place of honor in the family. A graying head is a symbol of wisdom and splendor (Proverbs 20:29)! It is Dottie's and my deepest conviction that part of God's plan in upholding the family is to *restore the role of grandparents to a place of esteem, so that God's grace and favor may flow from one generation to the next.*

> **In our season of life, we may not be calling all the shots anymore—but we can still support our grown children from the sidelines!**

Parenting is not an easy task. It is not a calling for the faint-hearted. The tyranny of life necessitates the support of extended families. Our grown children need our encouragement, our experience, and our active involvement in this most vital endeavor. They also need our availability to help with their young families and our willingness to lift some of the burden of child-rearing from their shoulders, whenever possible. We grandparents *can* make a difference! And we can accomplish this without undermining our children's role as parents in their own households. In our season of life, we may not be calling all the shots anymore—but we can still support our grown children from the sidelines!

Grandparenting is not a stroll down the Path of Perfection. It can, at times, be a bumpy journey along Reality Road. On this journey, there is plenty of room for us to make mistakes. Mistakes provide our greatest opportunities to learn! For any of us who may have gotten off to a rocky start on this journey of grandparenting, it is never too late to hit the "reset" button and start afresh. So be encouraged. God's mercy is new every morning. His grace will always compensate for our lack! *"Let us then approach God's throne of grace with confidence, so that we may receive mercy and find grace to help us in our time of need"* (Hebrews 4:16 NIV). The apostle Peter encourages us very simply: *"Love covers a multitude of sins"* (1 Peter 4:8 ESV). Knowing that our sins—and our mistakes—are completely forgiven and covered by the blood of Jesus gives us a peace and a confidence that the faithfulness of our heavenly Father will enable us to fulfill the special calling given to grandparents.

It is never too late to hit the "reset" button and start afresh.

If our children are a blessing from the Lord, then our grandchildren are a double portion of His blessing, and our great-grandchildren are a triple blessing! Would God give us this blessed calling as grandparents—and then abandon us to work it out on our own? Certainly not! God gives us his promised provision of all-sufficient grace. *"My grace is sufficient for you, for my power is made perfect in weakness"* (2 Corinthians 12:9 NIV). The Lord will equip us for the wonderful and rewarding role of grandparenting to which He has called us!

> *Now may the God of peace . . . equip you with everything good for doing his will, and may he work in us what is pleasing to him, through Jesus Christ, to whom be glory for ever and ever* (Hebrews 13:20–22 NIV).

With this new understanding from Scripture of the critical obligation grandparents bear to leave a righteous legacy for future generations, Dottie and I knew it was time for us to consider the legacy we would leave to our heirs.

We now shifted our focus to the most pressing question on our minds: *How do we begin to build a family legacy?*

OUR PRAYER

Dear Lord,

We are beginning to see that grandparenting is more than sitting back and observing our grandchildren's lives from the sidelines. We care so much about them and, especially, about their spiritual lives, yet we know that YOU love them even more than we do!

We pray for Your help to be an active model and a living testimony of Your love and forgiveness in the eyes of our grandchildren—and for Your grace to extend to them the same love and forgiveness that we have received from You.

May our grandchildren enjoy a personal relationship with You— not only to hear stories about You, but also to have Your presence abiding in their hearts. May Your blessing be upon them as they continue to mature in our wayward society.

In Your holy name we pray,

Amen.

3 · FAMILY IDENTITY:
WHO AM I ... REALLY?

For I know the plans I have for you, declares the LORD, plans for welfare and not for evil, to give you a future and a hope.
—Jeremiah 29:11 ESV

I t is innate in every human heart: the desire to know our identity or family roots. Whether we come from an intact home, or from a broken home, we were all born into a family identity of some sort. A legacy that is passed down from one generation to the next is a family's *identity*.

A recurring refrain we hear today is the catchphrase "identity crisis." Experiencing an identity crisis is the acceptable euphemism that rationalizes all sorts of quirky behaviors. *Why does she dye her hair magenta? Why does he hang out with that crowd? Why do we spend so much time and money trying to recapture our youthful appearances? Why do I feel like my life is going nowhere?* It is considered acceptable to justify such conduct with the explanation, "It's only an identity crisis. It will pass." The truth is, many of us *are* experiencing an identity crisis, in the truest sense of the expression.

The starting point for fashioning a family legacy is discovering our true identity. Regrettably, the reality is that many of us do not honestly or accurately know what our true identity is. We typically derive our identities from various worldly sources: our occupations, the size of our paychecks, where we live, how we dress, what kind of car we drive, our ethnic backgrounds, our successes, our failures, and so on. Not surprisingly, some of the strongest messages we hear about our identities come from our families. In order to truly understand our family identities, it's often helpful to take a look back at our formative years.

ROGER SHARES...

There was a time in my life when it would have been invaluable to have grandparents' shoulders to stand upon. I dearly wanted someone who could tell me stories about my mother and father, such as how they met, and where they grew up. But sadly, it was not to be.

I did not know anything about my family identity until I was eighteen years old. It was then that I was told my young, beautiful mother had died of spinal meningitis in 1939. She was only twenty-six years old, and I was three. My baby sister was only a month old when our mother died.

There was a time in my life when it would have been invaluable to have grandparents' shoulders to stand upon.

At the time, America was on the verge of war. My dad was a sailor and was seldom at home. With my father out to sea, I had become my mother's *little man*. I felt like a very important three-year-old. My mother was all I had—and then, abruptly, she was gone.

I remember attending my mother's funeral—the one who had been my life until that time. Seeing her casket lowered into the ground was more than I could handle, and my young heart and brain simply shut down. I went into shock. My father had to return to his duty at sea immediately after the funeral, so I was taken to the farm prison where my grandfather worked, to stay with my elderly grandparents. I recall my first day there, being sent outside to play, and when I asked where my mother was, the reply from the doorway was simply, "She is gone."

Then the door slammed shut—to the farm and to my heart. My mother was never mentioned again. Lonely and confused, I cried desperately for her.

I soon learned that any mention of my mother was something that I was expected to avoid. In compliance, I mentally brought closure to that season of my life.

My mother's parents were completely absent from my life. Curiously, before she died, she made my father promise never to let her own side of the family have anything to do with my sister and me. I never knew why. I never asked.

My father's parents felt they could not care for two young children, so my father had to continue searching for someone willing to care for us. My sister and I were transferred from one boarding house to another. Each time my father returned from sea, he found that he was not satisfied with our care, so he transferred us to yet another boarding house before returning to his ship.

I remember my heart aching—if only I had one grandparent who wanted me, a grandparent to whom I could feel an attachment.

I remember my heart aching—if only I had *one* grandparent who wanted me, a grandparent to whom I could feel an attachment. But that longing of a young boy's heart was not to be answered for many years—not until I discovered how deeply I was cherished by my heavenly Father.

Things were extremely difficult for my father. World War II was threatening, and he was in the Coast Guard. His division was fully occupied in the North Atlantic, guiding the supply ships that were bringing food and arms to England and protecting the supply ships from German submarines.

I grew up bewildered, vulnerable, and confused. I did not have anyone to guide me with answers to a child's most basic identity questions: *"Who am I?"* and *"Why am I here?"* The traumatic and sudden death of my mother affected me emotionally for many years, leaving my world fragmented.

When I was five years old, my father remarried—to an older woman almost fifteen years his senior. Compared to my memories of my young and beautiful mother, his new wife seemed absolutely *ancient.*

I did not have anyone to guide me with answers to a child's most basic identity questions: "Who am I?" and "Why am I here?"

All the joy in my early life utterly vanished. I rejected my stepmother for many years. Communication became extremely difficult for me. While I was thankful to at least have a home, my emotions had been buried along with my mother. It would take someone very special to awaken my heart from its protective slumber. Little did I know at that time that God already had a wonderful plan brewing for my good. For in the very year of my mother's death, many miles away, a little baby named Dorothy was born.

DOTTIE SHARES...

As I described in an earlier chapter, my upbringing and family identity were vastly different from Roger's experiences.

Although my mother's parents lived too far away to be involved in our daily lives, they did drive my two brothers and me to their camp in New Hampshire for week-long summer vacations. In addition to providing wonderful memories of my youth, these times spent with my grandparents also gave my parents a welcome vacation from us kids.

Nevertheless, my father's mother—affectionately known as *Ginnah* to her grandchildren—was my favorite. When I was a little girl,

Ginnah read me stories and taught me to play Gin Rummy and Double Solitaire. My stomach still relishes memories of her baked egg custard, and a pat of sweet, melted butter on one of her oven honey rolls was dinner enough. What a cook she was!

Ginnah was a great listener as well. In contrast to Roger's reserved manner of communication, I was a talker! And whenever I needed to talk, Ginnah was ready to listen. I could approach her with whatever was on my heart, and I never felt judged or demeaned by her.

I fondly recall one earth-shattering predicament that I brought to my grandmother for her wise advice. Somehow, the situation felt like a crisis to me at the time.

When I was a high school senior, a certain young man pursued me with intentions of marriage. I knew my parents disapproved of the early marriage, and in *their* minds, there was nothing more to discuss. Looking for an understanding ear, I turned to my grandmother. I knew she would listen benevolently to me. She herself had married my grandfather at the youthful age of eighteen—and for forty years, they had a successful and happy marriage.

Without one discouraging word of disapproval...my clever grandmother diplomatically pointed me back to one of my heart's desires.

As I anticipated, Ginnah did listen patiently while I presented my case, and then she shot one strategically aimed arrow at my logic, "My dear, I thought you wanted to be a teacher. You are so good with children. Why don't you go to college?" Without one discouraging word of disapproval over a premature marriage, my clever grandmother diplomatically pointed me back to one of my heart's desires. She was a wise woman.

Admittedly, I was not really ready for marriage. Marriage could wait.

The relationship with my young suitor ended, and in the fall, I entered college to become a teacher. My parents were thrilled. Ginnah had saved me from a monumental mistake. Little did she know how life-changing her advice would prove to be!

Roger and I had known each other growing up. He was like a brother to me. When I turned nineteen and had finished my first year of college, Roger made his move—and he hasn't moved since! For fifty-seven years, I have been married to my best friend. (Ironically, Roger wasn't the only one to make his move. My brother made his move also—and is now married to Roger's younger sister!) By the grace of God, the "M.R.S." degree I earned in college has been the most rewarding degree I could have earned. I am so grateful for the day that my grandmother took off her apron and listened to me. Without her I might have married the wrong man.

THOUGHTS TO PONDER

ROGER SHARES...

Some of you, like me, know what it is like to come from a painful past. We are not given the opportunity to choose the circumstances into which we were born. To be candid, some of us would not have chosen our circumstances if we had been given a choice. Yet we *can* choose how we respond to our circumstances. And we can choose to forgive those who have hurt us or let us down. We can choose to believe that God is sovereign and omnipresent, and therefore, He was present in every circumstance of our lives, both the good and the bad. We can trust that God is good, and that He always does what is for our ultimate good, even when circumstances make no sense to us. *"And we know that all things work together for good to those who love God, to those who are the called according to His purpose"* (Romans 8:28).

Although we neither know everything nor see everything clearly, yet we can still trust God at His word: *"For as the heavens are higher than the earth, so are My ways higher than your ways, and My thoughts than your thoughts"* (Isaiah 55:9). It is the Lord's plan all along that we should turn to Him to satisfy our longings and heal our hearts. The joys I have found in Jesus and in my wife, Dottie, are indescribable. I have found my identity—in Christ and in the joys of leading my family in the ways of the Lord. Without a doubt, the blessing of being the patriarch of a new family legacy is worth everything I once considered loss. When we ourselves have experienced healing, we become uniquely qualified to help others who are hurting.

We can choose to believe that God is sovereign and omnipresent, and therefore, He was present in every circumstance of our lives, both the good and the bad.

So, what is our identity *really?* The moment a person is converted, his or her identity for all eternity becomes *child of God,* beloved by our heavenly Father. *"You received the Spirit of adoption by whom we cry out, 'Abba, Father.' The Spirit Himself bears witness with our spirit that we are children of God"* (Romans 8:15–16). Our true identity is the Lord's adopted, chosen children. We are the inheritance He has promised to His own Son. We are His disciples. We are servants of the almighty God. We are not abandoned or left in confusion, as I was as a young man. No circumstances in this world can ever take away or tarnish the identity God has given us!

It was becoming more and more clear to us that the legacy we were to pass down to our children and grandchildren would be an imperishable inheritance. It would be a legacy of Jesus Himself, alive in us, and a legacy of faithfulness to God's eternal Word!

Having settled the question of our own identities, we turned our attention to the next perplexing question on our minds: *What practical things could we do that would demonstrate the life and love of Jesus in us to our grandchildren—to leave a lasting, positive legacy for our grandchildren?*

OUR PRAYER

Dear heavenly Father,

You are a kind God and care deeply about our past hurts and disappointments. Though we haven't always felt it, You have always been with us—in every circumstance in our lives. You are the God who heals the brokenhearted. You are the one who grants us new beginnings and gives us an identity that no power of man can ever extinguish. You are the God who restores beauty from ashes, who places a banner of love over us, who sets us as a seal upon Your own heart, and who adopts us as Your own children for all eternity! Help us to receive all that You delight to give us.

Thank you that You made a way for us to forgive those who have wounded us, as we ourselves have been forgiven by You. And thank you that You have made it possible for us to pass down a legacy of purity and wholeness to our children and grandchildren, untainted by bitter roots from the past.

In Jesus' name,

Amen.

4 • BEGINNING A FAMILY LEGACY

How great are His signs, and how mighty His wonders! His kingdom is an everlasting kingdom, and His dominion is from generation to generation.

—Daniel 4:3

All it takes to begin to fashion a family legacy is a simple, special memory that transcends generations—and you are on your way!

Roger and I started grandparenting when we were in our mid-forties. At that time, the thought of beginning a family legacy for grandchildren was the furthest thing from our minds. We expected that grandparenting would be a challenge, but we were confident that it could not be any harder than being a parent.

God's grace was amazing for a couple of relatively young, inexperienced grandparents like us. Without delay, He began to show us practical ways that we could demonstrate the love of Jesus to our children and grandchildren. We were about to embark on the joyful, rewarding ride of a lifetime, and thirteen grandchildren and sixteen great-grandchildren later, the train has not slowed down yet! Two more great-grandchildren are on the way! We chuckle now as we look back on our first days as novice grandparents.

I will never forget the surge of joy that filled my heart when my daughter Kimberly asked me to help with *her* daughter's first bath. Kim and her husband, Warren, were staying in our air-conditioned family room during an oppressive heat wave.

"Mom, I need your help," Kimberly called.

Those magical words were music to a new grandmom's ears. I was needed!

I felt honored that my daughter trusted me with her precious baby—but to be honest, I was also scared! Babies are so tiny—and *fragile!* I experienced one of those brain-freeze moments. It had been twenty-three years since I had bathed a baby. Could I remember how to do it? Not wanting my daughter to sense my insecurity, I tried to act confident. First, I prepared a bowl of warm water and laid out a fresh diaper. *So far so good; I had remembered the basics!* Next came a clean undershirt, a tiny gown, and a fluffy towel to dry and wrap baby Julie. Thankfully, all the essential baby skills came back to me once I got started—

There is no more powerful or effectual legacy you can leave to the next generations than that of a praying grandparent.

but what a challenging ordeal it was! At least I hadn't drowned my granddaughter in her first bath! Our budding family legacy was surely off to a good start.

A short time after our first granddaughter was born, our middle daughter, Robin, announced that she and her husband, Mike, were about to bless us with our second grandchild. In due time, Ben, our first grandson, arrived. As a seasoned grandmother of two now, bathing Ben was much less stressful for me. I was getting the hang of it again—and loving it! In the simplicity of living life together, our family bath-time legacy was forged.

When our third daughter, Lisa, started her family, I was blessed to be present at the births of three of her children. The baby I missed decided to arrive in the middle of a snowstorm. But neither snow nor storm could keep Grandmom away, and I arrived as soon as it was safe to make the three-hour trip. After all, it was important to keep the bath-time legacy flourishing!

More grandchildren continued to arrive. Our "quiver" was filling with young, lively "arrows." The arrival of each new baby marked another creative miracle from God. Gazing upon each unique little face brought the words of Psalm 139 to life: *"I praise you because I am fearfully and wonderfully made; your works are wonderful"* (Psalm 139:14 NIV).

Our grandchildren have come into our lives like thirteen little stepping stones. After Julie and Ben came Jeff and Matthew, followed by Amy and Kristie. They were the first cluster of six. We affectionately referred to them as *The Swarm.* Like a swarm of locusts clearing a field, they could swarm and devour a plate of fresh-baked chocolate chip cookies in no time.

Next to be added to our fast-growing brood were Andy, Kevin, and Grant. Three bottomless boys necessitated two plates of cookies. It was becoming a challenge to keep Grandma's freezer filled with cookies, casseroles, and ice cream for the gang!

Timothy, Melanie, Stephen, and Lianna brought up the third grouping of grandchildren. We called them *The Four Littles* because they were so much younger. To this day, even though they are grown, we still call them *The Four Littles.*

As new grandchildren were successively added to our family, our hearts grew larger and larger. Roger and I felt the urgency to press in to the Lord even more closely, asking Him to show us creative and meaningful ways to demonstrate the love of Jesus to all our little people.

CREATING A LEGACY OF PRAYER

Prayer. There is no more powerful or effectual legacy one can leave to the next generations than that of a praying grandparent. Right from the beginning of our own journey as grandparents, prayer has been our priority. We were inexperienced. We were novices. We needed wisdom from above. We found that grandparenting called us to continually battle our natural desires and subdue our impulsive inclinations. When we visited with our daughters' families, if we saw something about which we might have a different opinion, this became an opportunity to pray. *Whatever we observed with our eyes or heard with our ears became prayer on our knees.* Out of respect for the marriages of our daughters and sons-in-law and their autonomy in their own homes, we were careful to watch our words and restrain our impulses to offer unsolicited advice. Prayer was our only option. So we turned our cares into prayers.

One of the most challenging areas in building relationships with grown children is knowing when to speak—and when to refrain from speaking.

It was at this time that I started my family prayer journal. This journal was not only therapeutic and sanctifying for me, but it just might have been the saving grace that saved our family relationships! In this journal, I often talked to the Lord before I talked to my grown children. I was reminded that for everything there is a season (Ecclesiastes 3:1). There was a time to jump in and help my daughters; and there was a time to restrain my natural inclinations to help. I learned that not every thought that popped into my head necessarily needed to spring out of my mouth!

There were many occasions when I wanted to offer my daughters advice, particularly in the area of discipline. After all, hadn't I earned that right by virtue of having lived so many years on earth? As much as my instincts were to help by giving unsolicited advice, I learned that some of my well-meaning words were likely to sow seeds of discord—not peace—in the family. Many will agree with me when I say that one of the most challenging areas in building relationships with grown children is knowing when to speak—and when to refrain from speaking. While this may sound extremely basic, I simply had to learn when to keep my mouth shut—and I was a slow learner! The Lord, however, has been a kind Teacher, quick to forgive and gracious to install a holy and discerning zipper on my lips!

As our family grew, the Lord gave me another delightful idea for a simple, yet significant, legacy of prayer. In my journal, I began to write a prayer for each family member on his or her birthday. I limited each prayer to one page—but that was sufficient to express my heart. Birthdays became a very special time for me to lift individual family members before the Lord's throne of grace and commemorate them in a personal prayer. Today, I still write personal birthday prayers for my twenty-eight grandchildren and great-grandchildren, in addition to my daughters and sons-in-law.

The most special part of this legacy of prayer is that I have kept my prayer journal private—just between my heavenly Father and myself. My little lambs will be able to read my prayers for them after I am on the other side of eternity. What a day that will be—when my legacy of prayer is passed on to the next generation! By then, my children, grandchildren, and great-grandchildren may already have seen how my prayers for them have been answered!

With so many children among whom to divide our time, it has taken some planning to design special time with each child individually.

CREATING A LEGACY VACATION

We all know what a priceless treasure it is to spend quality time with loved ones. Those of us who experienced this can attest to the precious memories we have from childhood. Those who missed this opportunity, like Roger, might have an even greater appreciation for quality family time. What a blessing it has been for Roger to redeem his past childhood memories by playing an active role in creating new family memories for his own children and grandchildren. It's not surprising that many of the strongest memories that have defined our family identity center around spending quality time together with our grandchildren. We're not sure who enjoys our times together more—the grandchildren or us! Roger and I have reaped as much joy and youthful energy from these times as the children have. In fact, we may have discovered the secret to the Fountain of Youth: *grandchildren!*

With so many children among whom to divide our time, it has taken some planning to design special time with each child individually. But it has been well worth the effort! Out of our desire to spend quality one-on-one time with each grandchild has emerged one of our most cherished family traditions: *legacy vacations.*

It would be a great opportunity to share with our granddaughter our family heritage and impart to her a sense of her own identity—in a fun way.

Turning a vacation into a legacy is a tradition we began when little Julie was nine years old. At the time, she was quite interested in our family history, so Roger and I proposed the spontaneous idea of taking Julie to visit the places where he and I grew up in New England. Her parents agreed that it would be a great opportunity to share with our granddaughter our family heritage and impart to her a sense of her own identity—in a fun way.

Our destination was my grandparents' camp along the shore of a scenic New Hampshire lake, nestled in the pine trees and offering plenty of hiking trails. Our plan was to take Julie to spend a long weekend with my folks.

Our first stop along the way was Connecticut, to visit Great-Great-Grandma Robinson, who lived in a nursing home. She was still in amazing health. At ninety-eight years old, she thought that the Lord might have forgotten her, but she was still full of life and interesting conversation!

To capture the moment, we had our video camera in hand, and we encouraged Julie to ask Great-Great-Grandma any questions that were on her mind:

"Where did you grow up?"

"How old are you?"

"What was school like in a one-room schoolhouse?"

"Did you have a television when you grew up?"

"How old were you when you got married?"

"Do you know Jesus?"

Unfortunately, only our three oldest grandchildren—Julie, Ben, and Jeff—had the opportunity to spend time with Great-Great-Grandma Robinson before she went home to be with her Savior at the age of 101.

The next stop was my hometown in Massachusetts. During my childhood years, it had been a small, quaint country town with a population of a mere 1,200. It was a town where everyone knew each other. Roger, Julie, and I visited the elementary school where my third and fourth grade teachers had both taught my own father thirty-five years earlier. My teachers' memories of my father had not helped me to gain their affections one bit. My father and his friends were notorious for putting cherry bombs in the boys' lavatories and getting themselves expelled from school.

Not far from the school was the Congregational Church where Roger and I were married. It was fun to share our love story with our grandchildren. Even the boys were amused. From the church, we traveled four miles out of town, across the railroad tracks to Bruce Street, where I grew up. My childhood home, an old twelve-room farmhouse, was still standing, although it now belonged to new owners. The owners were kind enough to let us explore with Julie. Upstairs, I was surprised to discover that the floor in the bathroom, although a bit worn, still had the same sparkled paint that my mother had painted it fifty years before. Even the four-legged bathtub was still in use.

Around the corner from the bathroom was my childhood bedroom. I did not remember its being so small, especially my closet, but back then we didn't own many clothes.

Down in the cellar, we discovered the preserve closet that my father had built for my mother's summer canning. We could hardly believe our eyes—there on a shelf sat an old pint of dill pickles dated *1952*. We brought it up and gave it to the owners. We were not brave enough to sample the decades-old pickles!

The experience of vacationing together has been so memorable that, even today, as our grandchildren are grown and some have children of their own, we have continued this legacy.

It was sad to see that the barn where my brothers and I had played was torn down. But Julie still enjoyed my stories about playing hide-and-seek in the hayloft with my brothers and swinging treacherously from a rope, jumping recklessly into the hay. What fun we used to have—and now we had the joy of sharing our memories with our granddaughter!

We ended our nostalgic trip by indulging in one of the privileges of being a grandparent: sharing with Julie the simple pleasure of a huge banana split at the ice cream stand where I had worked fifty years earlier to earn money for college.

Driving home from our long weekend, Roger took the opportunity to share with Julie about *his* hometown. It had been a mill town about twenty miles from my home. Roger admitted that he did not have much to share, but even so, he has a wonderful way of spinning stories from even the sparsest details. Roger told wide-eyed Julie how he and his buddies used to meet at the swimming hole, where they would hang out until dinnertime, or until the water shriveled their skin like raisins. One of Roger's favorite stories to tell the grandchildren was the story of his BB-gun escapades. He and one of his buddies shot BB holes into all the paint cans in his buddy's grandfather's barn. What fun they had shooting holes and watching the paint colors mix—until they were caught. Then, the guilty boys had to pay for their crime by cleaning up the colossal paint mess. Even though Roger's hometown did not mean much to him, he discovered that it *did* mean something to our grandchild. Julie could feel content and secure. Pop-Pop had a home, too.

They certainly get the message that they are loved and valued!

The experience of vacationing together has been so memorable that, even today, as our grandchildren are grown and some have children of their own, we have continued this legacy. Roger, our sons-in-law, and our grandsons climb mountain trails and brave the wilderness together. But that is a story for a later chapter.

PASSING DOWN A LEGACY OF PORTRAITS

ROGER SHARES...

Dottie and I have greatly desired that our grandchildren would grow up knowing the love and acceptance of the Lord through us. We were thrilled when the Lord gave us an idea to demonstrate that love in a very tangible way. Although this seems like a very simple idea, it has become a wonderful legacy in our family. We created an attractive wall of photographs on a prominent wall in our kitchen. Arranged by family, a portrait of each of our grandchildren is featured on this wall of photos. Our daughters are responsible for keeping us up to date with their children's current pictures. Not only does our wall of young, cheerful faces add warm ambiance to the whole kitchen, but it also grants us "bragging rights" when visitors come to our home! We view that as another one of those grandparent privileges! Most importantly, our wall of portraits has a special place in the hearts of our grandchildren. We have been amazed at the number of times one of our grandchildren has come into the kitchen and commented on his or her picture. They certainly get the message that they are loved and valued!

We are all familiar with the adage that a picture is worth a thousand words. There are so many ways to communicate meaningful messages with pictures. Another one of Dottie's picture projects was creating individual photo albums, each featuring one of our grandchildren, to document milestones in their lives. Along with these photo albums, Dottie tucked the child's precious letters printed in childish handwriting into scrapbooks.

It is becoming more and more clear to us that the legacy we impart to our grandchildren is an imperishable legacy.

A lasting legacy is already emerging as we watch our grandchildren reminisce over their albums, together with their cousins, giggling and laughing as they recall the events surrounding the pictures. But alas, having begun with good intentions, we have not been able to keep up the scrapbooking. Thirteen grandchildren have spawned pictures and memories faster than Dottie can create scrapbooks! Looking nostalgically at boxes filled with warm keepsakes, she can only sigh, *"Maybe one day . . . "*

Speaking of pictures, our grandchildren love to learn about their heritage by looking at heirloom family photos, faded images worn at the edges but resilient to the effects of time. On a wall leading upstairs, we have arranged pictures of the generations. In fact, the oldest photo on the wall is a picture of Dottie's great-great-grandmother. It is about 130 years old! Each one of these heirloom pictures has a story to tell. Our grandchildren never seem to tire of hearing their family stories.

We even have a picture of my mother and father standing together with me. This picture has given me opportunities to keep the stories alive of how my mother died, where I was sent to live, and how God cared for me during that season in my life. We always end our family story times with Dottie's and my wedding photos and our love story. The children are entranced by the wonderful story of how God brought Dottie and me together.

It is becoming more and more clear to us that the legacy we impart to our grandchildren is an *imperishable* legacy. It is the legacy of Jesus Himself, His eternal Word, and His divine plan for multigenerational families—whether natural children or children grafted into our family by God. We trust that the time we spend with our grandchildren and the stories we pass on to them will continue to impart to them a stronger sense of God's divine plan for *who* they are, *where* they have come from, and *why* they are here. As they grow in their faith, they will come to understand their greatest purpose in this life is to glorify God and to pass the gospel message on to the generations that follow.

> **Whether you know it or not, you already have begun to create a legacy.**

THOUGHTS TO PONDER

You might be thinking, "We would love to create a legacy for our grandchildren, but how do we begin?"

Whether you know it or not, you already have begun to create a legacy. Perhaps the shoulders of the previous generation that you were given to stand upon appear to have failed you. But the good news is, *God never fails us.*

With your eyes fixed on Jesus, you will not fail either. He makes all things new (Revelation 21:5). Jesus will build into your family strong shoulders to stand upon, for the second, third, and fourth generations, and beyond. Your legacy will be one of your greatest gifts to the generations that follow in your footsteps.

God may not have literal grandchildren, but *our grandchildren can have our God!* He is the pearl of great worth that we leave to them.

Before moving forward with our story, in the next chapter we will take a step back in time—back to the place where it all begins.

OUR PRAYER

Dear heavenly Father,

You have never left us without family or an identity. You have adopted us and called us Your children. And You have loved us, more than any earthly father could ever love his children. Your love is deep and abiding. It never fails.

Thank you for entrusting to us the gift of grandchildren. What a blessing and a delight their young lives are! We pray that You will teach us our role in their lives as grandparents. Open our eyes to see the wonderful plans You have for each of them. Equip us to leave them a legacy that honors You.

We entrust our grandchildren into Your capable hands, for we know that Your love for them is far greater than our human love could ever be.

We ask You these things in the name of Jesus.

Amen.

5 • IT ALL BEGINS WITH DYING

Truly, truly, I say to you, unless a grain of wheat falls into the earth and dies, it remains alone; but if it dies, it bears much fruit.
—John 12:24 ESV

efore we continue on our journey into grandparenting, we would like to pause and share one of the chief obstacles that could have hindered us from passing on a godly legacy to our heirs: what we refer to as our *self-life*. It took Roger and me many years, though, before we actually understood what that concept meant. I still recall a little poem my mother used to recite to me, called "Three Guests" by Jessica Nelson North:

I had a little tea party
This afternoon at three.
'Twas very small—
Three guests in all—
Just I, myself and me.
Myself ate all the sandwiches,
While I drank up the tea;
'Twas also I who ate the pie
And passed the cake to me.

At the time, I did not understand what Mother's poem meant. It was just a cute little ditty. But in 1970, when Roger and I first heard the gospel message, the words of Mother's little poem suddenly sprang to life, and we understood their meaning for the first time. We realized that Mother's lyrics described *us*. Our worlds revolved around *ourselves*, as if *we* were the honored guests at our own tea party. Like Satan in the garden of Eden, vying to be like God, we were proud, self-absorbed, and living our lives according to our own agenda, believing we knew what was best. We had no problem identifying with Adam as he gave in to the temptation to eat from the Tree of Knowledge and thus become like God. Ever since Adam gave in to that temptation, the desires of the hearts of mankind have been waging war against the perfect will of God. Adam passed down a legacy to all of us from the Tree of Knowledge—trusting in our own understanding, to do what seems right in our own myopic eyes. The older we become, the more aware we are of the many times our human nature longs to have its own way! The natural outworking is our inclination to strive to be in control of situations.

The Lord has been so kind to teach us through His Word that the only way to really live is to be willing to die— die to our self-life.

When the Lord called us to surrender our lives to Him, Roger and I knew we needed to lay down control of our lives. It was time to give up doing things our way and begin doing things God's way. His ways, after all, are higher than our ways. His ways are perfect! I was the first to drop to my knees and ask the Lord's forgiveness for leaving Him out of the picture and living a life that digressed from His holiness. A few short months later, Roger, too, responded to the gospel call. As we repented of our sinful ways and laid our lives at the feet of Jesus, an amazing thing happened—we were *born again!* Instantly, we received a new nature that glorified Jesus Christ. Our natural, sinful, human nature that we inherited from Adam was put to death, figuratively, and in its place, we were raised, by faith, to newness of life in Jesus Christ. Jesus himself tells us,

> *Most assuredly, I say to you, unless one is born again, he cannot see the kingdom of God* (John 3:3).

> *Just as Christ was raised from the dead by the glory of the Father, even so we also should walk in newness of life* (Romans 6:4).

> *Therefore, if anyone is in Christ, he is a new creation; old things have passed away; behold, all things have become new* (2 Corinthians 5:17).

What a life-changing gift of salvation the Lord gave us in that season of our lives! At long last, our "tea party of three" became an audience of One! From that moment on, our one true desire has been to live lives worthy of the calling of Christ Jesus, the cause for which He gave His life.

In the years since then, the Lord has been so kind to teach us through His Word that the only way to really live is to be willing to die—die to our self-life. We are called to live by the Spirit (Romans 8:14) and to relinquish those subtle vestiges of self-seeking desire that lurk in our hearts. Thanks be to God—who has set us free from the need to pursue our own agendas! *"For the law of the Spirit of life in Christ Jesus has made me free from the law of sin and death"* (Romans 8:2). Now, we are truly free to do as Jesus admonishes us: love and serve one another, as He has done for us.

THE "KINGDOM OF SELF" STARTS YOUNG

"Did I hear correctly? Where on earth did THAT comment come from?" I was shocked by the melodramatic scene I had just observed. Sweet little Julie—only three years old—was just learning to speak her mind.

And was she ever doing an eloquent job of expressing herself. There was little doubt that Julie had *my* genes in her!

It was the summer of 1983, and our family was vacationing together in the peaceful woods of New Hampshire. Julie was the center of much attention. As our first grandchild, she had her parents, her grandparents, and her great-grandparents to dote upon her. We all adored her.

One evening at bedtime, when her parents called her to get ready for bed, Julie stood in the middle of the room with her hands firmly on her hips. From her angelic little mouth floated a youthful display of her innate sin nature: *"I don't want anyone to tell me what to do."* There was no doubt that Julie's young self-life wanted to be in control. Only through firm parenting and the grace of God did Julie surrender her will in obedience to her parents that night. There was no doubt that the seeds of Adam were alive and kicking in *our* offspring!

Let's face it; each one of us has myriad opportunities to choose between doing what serves our own desires and denying ourselves in deference to serving others.

When Julie became a teenager, we rejoiced to witness the transformation of her heart and her life as she responded to the gospel call and surrendered her life to the lordship of Jesus Christ. Julie's desire to live her life her own way, apart from God, was nailed to the cross once and for all, and Jesus became her personal Savior. Julie is now the mother of three precious little ones of her own! We pray that this legacy continues and that our great-grandchildren will surrender their lives to their Savior in the Lord's perfect timing.

Let's face it; each one of us has myriad opportunities to choose between doing what serves our own desires and denying ourselves in deference to serving others. Our contemporary culture offers an alluring array of family images and lifestyles for those of us who have reached our Golden Years. We are bombarded with messages that the Golden Years are our time to enjoy life, to relax, to travel, to remodel—in short, to indulge in the pleasures we denied ourselves while we were raising children. But *cultural* messages are sometimes *counterfeit* messages for God's perfect design—promising us lasting happiness, but failing to deliver on that promise. Few things are genuinely as fulfilling as kneeling beside a grandchild to pray together; few things are as memorable as baiting a makeshift fishing hook together with a grandchild, and a worm that is struggling to wiggle free from its fate; and few things are as rewarding as being present to celebrate a grandchild's first field goal, or to be available to lend a listening ear when a grandchild opens a window into his or her heart.

> **We are bombarded with messages that the Golden Years are our time to enjoy life, to relax, to travel, to remodel—in short, to indulge in the pleasures we denied ourselves while we were raising children.**

We do not often hear the honest message of the deep and authentic implications of the cross of Christ and the outworking of it in our lives, but that message is one that calls us to die to our self-lives daily, to surrender our personal desires for the sake of serving others. That may be an unpopular, uncomfortable message to absorb. We rarely speak of the cost of being a disciple of Christ. Yet, Jesus himself tells us that being his disciple will cost us our very lives:

> *Then Jesus said to his disciples, "Whoever wants to be my disciple must deny themselves and take up their cross and follow me. For whoever wants to save their life will lose it, but whoever loses their life for me will find it"* (Matthew 16:24 NIV).

A godly family legacy begins with dying. We believe families are God's ordained backdrop to teach us to die daily. Family life certainly gives us plenty of opportunities in the course of a day! Again and again, we are reminded that the "old man" dies hard. But we have to remember, too, that we are a new creation, clothed in the righteousness of God's Son; and that is what God the Father sees when He looks at us—not the old man we once were as heirs of Adam. We are so grateful that the Lord encourages us and helps us to live righteously and does not condemn us when we fall short. His forgiveness is a powerful tool in our grandparenting tool chest. His patience far exceeds ours!

As grandparents, there are many times when our own desires or routines or comfort clash with serving our children and grandchildren.

As grandparents, there are many times when our own desires or routines or comfort clash with serving our children and grandchildren. Life itself can be complicated and messy. Add grandchildren into the picture, and the potential for conflict is compounded. An unwanted tug-of-war may erupt in our hearts over who gets to spend time with a grandchild—the in-laws or us! The old self, the one we thought was dead, suddenly springs back to life, and the war between the Spirit and the flesh wages on. But more about that in a later chapter.

Lastly, we want to be clear that there is nothing inherently wrong with relaxing or enjoying our lives and our homes in our post-child-rearing years. These are good gifts from the Lord and are among the blessings of life. At the same time, it is prudent not to mistake the counterfeit models of happiness put forth by our culture for the *real deal*. The real deal calls us to deny ourselves, lay down our lives, and do what Jesus would have admonished us to do: love and serve others. *That* is where the greatest joys of grandparenting will be found!

DOTTIE'S STORY . . .

Roger was serving as an officer in the Navy when we were first married. While he was out to sea, I returned to my parents' home in New England to have our firstborn child. That meant living with my mom and dad and grandparents, all under one roof. Imagine the scene: one kitchen accommodating three generations of women—with a fourth generation on the way!

I remember being in the kitchen one morning shortly after our baby was born, with activity bustling all around. I was attempting to care for my newborn daughter; my mother was scurrying around the cramped kitchen fixing breakfast for everyone, while simultaneously tending to my father's needs. Mother was in her usual rush, feeling the pressure to make it out the door on time for her job as a schoolteacher. In the midst of the chaos, Grandma Leavitt meandered into the kitchen, getting in my mother's way and oblivious to the frantic activity around her. I still remember my grandmother standing in the middle of the kitchen, hands on hips (a stance we women never seem to outgrow), inquiring, "Ain't I goin' to get nothin' to eat this morning?"

Many of us, young and old alike, approach family life as if it were designed to meet our own personal needs.

That was Grammy's way. She did this often. Poor Grammy. In her later years, she had forgotten how to cook, so my mother did all the cooking for everyone. In Grammy's blissful, childlike world, she could not see past the satisfaction of her own needs. We laugh about it now because of the pure, innocent childishness of it all. But the truth is that many of us, young and old alike, approach family life as if it were designed to meet our own personal needs. It follows that the closer and more comfortable we are with our families, the more prone we are to expect them to fulfill our needs.

Paradoxically, the logical place to begin our legacy as grandparents is where most stories end. True living begins with dying. There is simply no other way in God's design. *Unless a grain falls into the ground and dies, it cannot bear much fruit.* Dying is one of the most powerful and beautiful metaphors for the life of a believer. It represents our daily choices to identify with Jesus and His death and to allow Him to live through us. When Jesus walked the road to Calvary, He withheld nothing from us, but willingly gave Himself up to death for us. In a figurative sense, we are to do the same.

Love and serve others. That is where the greatest joys of grandparenting will be found!

What a legacy we can pass on to our children and grandchildren! We can be set free from our natural tendency to focus on our own needs and desires. We can be free to serve others selflessly. *"The Spirit of life in Christ Jesus has made me free from the law of sin and death"* (Romans 8:2). We cannot accomplish this amazing work ourselves. It is a miraculous work of the Holy Spirit in us that continues to transform us into the image and likeness of Jesus. God does not have an agenda to merely upgrade the "old man" of sin. The old man is already dead, nailed to the cross with Christ. *"For we know that our old self was crucified with him so that the body ruled by sin might be done away with"* (Romans 6:6 NIV). *"Likewise you, also, reckon yourselves to be dead indeed to sin, but alive to God in Christ Jesus our Lord"* (Romans 6:11).

God's desire is to utterly transform the "new man" in Christ so that everything about us reflects the selfless glory of our Savior. *"Just as Christ was raised from the dead through the glory of the Father, we too may live a new life"* (Romans 6:4 NIV).

Our only hope of leaving a godly legacy to our future generations is found in the legacy that Jesus Christ Himself left for us—accomplishing through His death, burial, and resurrected life what we could never accomplish for ourselves. It may have all begun with Adam in the garden, but it ended on the cross—where Jesus died to exchange our sinful humanity for His love.

> *And you also were included in Christ when you heard the message of truth, the gospel of your salvation. When you believed, you were marked in him with a seal, the promised Holy Spirit, who is a deposit guaranteeing our inheritance until the redemption of those who are God's possession—to the praise of his glory* (Ephesians 1:13–14 NIV).

OUR PRAYER

Dear heavenly Father,

We so desire to know more and more of who You are in the power of Your resurrection and the fellowship of Your sufferings, being conformed to Your death (Philippians 3:10). We realize that our old man keeps trying in vain to fix itself, when it is already dead. We need Your help to accept ourselves as You accept us: forgiven, redeemed, and clothed in the righteousness of Your Son. Sometimes that is so hard to comprehend; yet it is the truth. You are changing us from one degree of glory to another as we fix our gaze upon You.

Please forgive us, Lord, for trying so hard, in our own strength, to change our old man, dead in trespasses and sin. We need eyes to see that what is dead in Christ is truly dead. We need not strive so hard; we simply need You to transform us. We are so grateful that You see us clothed in the righteous garments of your Son Jesus. Your desire is to shower us with Your overflowing love—love that is all-powerful, unchanging, and irresistible—unlike any human love.

It is the desire of our hearts, Father, that our grandchildren would come to know You as You are—being neither independent of You nor legalistically dutiful. May they come to know You as a tender-hearted and merciful Father, and may they serve You with hearts that have been touched by Your Spirit in a personal way.

Your ways are ways of pleasantness, and all Your paths are peace. You are a Tree of Life to those who take hold of You (Proverbs 3:17–18).

We come to You in the name of Jesus.

Amen.

6 • A LEGACY OF LIVING FAITH

But be doers of the word, and not hearers only, deceiving your-
selves. . . . But he who looks into the perfect law of liberty and con-
tinues in it, and is not a forgetful hearer but a doer of the work,
this one will be blessed in what he does.

—James 1:22–25

The sun rose early that morning, promising a brilliant, warm day ahead. The fresh scent of nature wafted in through open windows. It was the kind of morning when one longs to linger in bed, relishing the delicious aroma of New England air and the tranquil sounds of nature. This was a vacation our family had been looking forward to. While I entertained the enticing thought of sleeping in, a certain seven-year-old young man was entertaining other plans—fishing!

It was very early in the morning when I happened to gaze out the window. There stood our grandson Ben with fishing net in one hand and a pole in the other. Heading for the wharf, Ben had only one thing on his young mind—*minnows!* Little did he know the living lesson of faith that the Lord had planned for him that morning.

Desiring to squeeze out a few more pleasant drops of sleep, I almost missed the amazing drama that was about to unfold. I roused myself from bed, dressed quietly, and strolled to the dock to see what Ben was up to. As I drew closer, I was surprised to see a downcast expression clouding his normally sunny face. *That's odd,* I thought. *I wonder if something has gone wrong.* I picked up my pace a bit.

Wanting to appear upbeat, I called out hopefully, "Any luck, Ben?"

"No, Mom-Mom," he moped. "I didn't catch any fish this morning. And Daddy and I need minnows for our fishing today."

Immediately, I thought of a familiar Bible story about a fisherman. This was a golden opportunity to show Ben that *living* faith is more than stories from past history—gospel faith is real and relevant to our lives today.

This was a golden opportunity to show Ben that living faith is more than stories from past history—gospel faith is real and relevant to our lives today.

Hoping to encourage him in his own budding faith, I began, "Ben, remember the time when Jesus came upon his disciples trying to fish, just like you? They had been fishing all night but hadn't caught a thing. When Jesus saw them struggling with their empty net, what did he tell the disciples to do?"

Ben perked up. "Jesus told them to cast their net on the other side of the boat, and they would catch some fish."

"That's exactly right, Ben."

Ben began to grow excited. He eagerly finished the story, "The disciples did what Jesus told them to do, and their net was so full of fish that they could hardly drag it in! Even with all those heavy fish in it, the net didn't even break." Ben was starting to see that faith in Jesus could come alive in very real ways in his life. He asked eagerly, " Mom-Mom, do you think Jesus will do the same for me?"

"I bet he would, Ben, if we ask Him. He loves to provide for His people. But we are the ones who neglect to ask Him for help when we should. Jesus was with the disciples when they needed His help to catch fish for their breakfast, and He's right here with you, too. Jesus is the same yesterday and forever. Let's go to Him and ask Him for some minnows right now, shall we?"

Ben bowed his head and prayed earnestly, "Dear Jesus, will You please bring some minnows, so Daddy and I can go fishing?"

It was a simple prayer from a young heart of faith. I agreed with Ben's prayer, and then we waited. Ben ran to the other side of the wharf, just like the disciples had done, and dipped his net quickly into the water.

Holding my breath, I cautioned for Ben's sake, "We must be patient and wait on the Lord. He doesn't always answer our prayers in the way that we expect Him to, but He *will* answer in His time."

To our utter amazement, the Lord released a whole school of minnows from under the wharf. Ben's fishing net was quickly filled—more than enough to fish for the whole day!

Planting a few seeds of living faith cost me nothing but a few extra minutes of sleep and a willingness to enter into a grandchild's world.

"WOW, Mom-Mom!" exclaimed Ben in wonder. "Did you see *that?!* There must be *thousands* of minnows. Jesus heard my prayer!"

Our jubilant rejoicing on the dock soon awakened the rest of the family. It was an amazing, faith-building moment for Ben. Did he ever have a story to share with the family! I have to admit that my own faith was strengthened as well that morning—by a little seven-year-old boy, a simple prayer of faith, and a Savior who is faithful to answer.

Ben is now thirty years old with three children of his own, yet the memory of that brief, simple prayer together on the dock remains one of his strongest childhood memories. Planting a few seeds of living faith cost me nothing but a few extra minutes of sleep and a willingness to enter into a grandchild's world.

If you profess a personal faith in Jesus, your role as a grandparent is more important than you may realize. The eyes of your grandchildren are watching you and taking in everything about you. One of the most precious gifts you can give them is the legacy of a living faith. Your testimony of living faith will leave a deep impression on your grandchildren as they see how profoundly your life has been affected by the power of Jesus' sacrificial death on Calvary. Let them see through simple acts of faith in your life that Jesus is alive today and is still doing wondrous works for people through the Holy Spirit.

MIMI IS MISSING

It was a crisp winter evening, and Julie was at a basketball game watching her daddy coach the team. Seated next to her on the bleachers was Mimi, Julie's favorite doll. At four years old, Julie and Mimi were inseparable. Mimi went everywhere with her. For all the affection Julie showered on Mimi, it was almost as if she were a real baby.

If you profess a personal faith in Jesus, your role as a grandparent is more important than you may realize.

As the game ended, Julie reached for Mimi. But her beloved baby doll was missing, nowhere to be found. Fear led to hysteria as a quick search in the obvious places for her doll turned up fruitless.

"Where's my Mimi?" Julie wailed, as only a brokenhearted little girl can wail. "Mimi is lost. She's run away. We can't go home without her."

By then, our family had formed a spontaneous search party, looking high and low for Mimi. Perhaps she had fallen under the bleachers or was left in the bathroom? But thorough searches of both places were futile. Mimi was hopelessly lost. By that point, Daddy was exhausted from a long day and wanted to go home.

"Daddy, we *can't* go home yet," Julie cried desperately. "We *have* to find my Mimi first!"

Daddy tried to show compassion and persevered in the search a while longer, but Mimi was, after all, only a doll, and his need for sleep at that point was *real*. Sleep did not come easily that night for our grieving little princess.

A whole week passed and still no sign of Mimi. Babysitting Julie one afternoon, I had the opportunity to talk to her about her lost doll as we had a tea party together. Mimi's place at the table was empty. My heart ached for Julie's loss, and I wanted her to know that Jesus cared about every detail of her life, and that faith in Him is a living faith.

Let them see through simple acts of faith in your life that Jesus is alive today and is still doing wondrous works for people through the Holy Spirit.

"Julie," I began. "I know how much you miss Mimi. I love Mimi, too. Why don't we pray together and ask Jesus to find her?"

"That won't work, Mom-Mom. Mimi is hiding."

"Julie, if anyone can find Mimi, Jesus can. He is a *big* Savior, and He is present everywhere. He sees *everything always*. No one can hide from Jesus—not even Mimi."

Julie prayed a simple prayer. "Dear Jesus, please find Mimi for me and bring her home. I miss her." We then continued with our tea party.

A couple of days later, I decided to tidy up a closet in our family room, which we had turned into a small playhouse for the grandchildren. In it were pots and pans, a small stove, a refrigerator, a crib, play food, a few dolls, building blocks and trucks for the boys.

As I opened the closet door, my eyes fixated in disbelief on an unexpected sight. There sat Mimi in a highchair! Or was it *really* Mimi?

How could it be? I had seen her with my own eyes at the basketball game. Besides, Julie would never have left Mimi at my house. She never went anywhere without Mimi.

Almost breathless with excitement, I called my daughter and asked if I could come over after Julie's nap. Time ticked by slowly as both my anticipation and my bewilderment grew.

God does answer prayers in peculiar ways, especially the prayers of His little ones.

When I arrived at my daughter's home, Julie was waiting for me. I held Mimi concealed behind my back, waiting for the right moment to surprise her.

"Mom-Mom?" asked Julie curiously. "What are you holding behind your back?"

Slowly I brought out Mimi. Julie's eyes lit up with joy. "Mimi!" she cried. "Where have you been? I've been looking all over for you, and Jesus found you! I don't ever want you to leave me again," Julie soberly chastised her baby doll in her best maternal voice.

To this day I don't know how Mimi appeared in the play closet. All I know is that the one who was once lost had now been found. Perhaps it was an angel who put her there. God does answer prayers in peculiar ways, especially the prayers of His little ones. The important thing was that Mimi was home again, and Julie knew that Jesus had heard and answered her prayer. Mimi remained Julie's favorite doll for many years—until the time came to pack her away for Julie's own children.

LIVING THE GOSPEL

A faith-filled life is not a life characterized by rules that must be followed or a list of things we ought or ought not do. The faith-filled life is a life that *radiates the love of God*. As grandparents, we have the unrivaled opportunity to model a living gospel before our grandchildren.

We can make the good news of God's love for mankind come alive in the eyes of our grandchildren!

Regretfully, Roger and I have not always lived our faith as spotlessly as we wish we had. A visible evidence of living the gospel is admitting to our grandchildren when we have made mistakes and asking their forgiveness. Children tend to personalize events in their lives, and if we don't take responsibility for our mistakes, children have a tendency to blame themselves. Allow us to share an example from our own family.

During one particular evening of babysitting, our patience with our grandchildren had been stretched to the limit. The children had been having a grand time playing, and evidence of their enjoyment was strewn all over the family room. Admittedly, we were worn out ourselves and were looking forward to guiding the children to bed.

A faith-filled life is not a life characterized by rules that must be followed or a list of things we ought or ought not do. The faith-filled life is a life that radiates the love of God.

"Okay, kids. It's clean-up time. Please pick up your toys and put them away."

That was the normal routine. On this night, however, our usual instructions fell on deaf ears as the children continued playing.

"Children! It's time to clean up your toys."

Still no response. At that point, we could have simply cleaned up the toys ourselves and communicated the situation to our daughter and son-in-law at the end of the evening. Instead, we were controlled by our desire to hustle the children to bed quickly and efficiently. So we became impatient with them—and we let it show.

"*Kids*—we have told you once, and we're not telling you again. *Pick up your toys,*" we emphatically enunciated each syllable. Our impatience was growing shamefully obvious.

Perhaps you're thinking, "What's so bad about telling children to clean up their toys?"

But there was a problem. The problem was our impatient state of heart and abrupt tone of voice in speaking to our much-loved grandchildren. In response, our grandchildren *did* stop their playing. The older child began to clean up toys—and the younger one began to cry. Talk about feeling remorseful. Seeing our grandchild's eyes well up with tears melted our hearts as the Spirit of God began to convict us.

We quickly saw that our impatience was not *living* the gospel of love before the children's eyes. We knew that we needed to confess our wrong behavior to them and ask them to forgive us.

> **We quickly saw that our impatience was not living the gospel of love before the children's eyes.**

"Mom-Mom and Pop-Pop are so sorry for the wrong way we spoke to you children tonight. We were feeling upset and impatient when you did not obey us. But we love you too much to hurt you with our words. We are very sorry. Will you forgive us for treating you unkindly?"

We were wrong in the way we treated the children, and by admitting it and asking their forgiveness, we demonstrated to them the living lesson that *we have need of a Savior.* As we might have anticipated, our grandchildren were quite willing to forgive us and restore our relationship. After baths, a story, a goodnight hug, and a prayer, the children promised to try harder to obey the next time. They fell asleep peacefully, knowing that Jesus loves and forgives Pop-Pops and Mom-Moms, too!

> *But God demonstrates His own love toward us, in that while we were still sinners, Christ died for us* (Romans 5:8).

THOUGHTS TO PONDER

Living our faith has been one of our greatest challenges. It is often a temptation, as adults, to send children the message, "Do as we say, not as we do." We have been amazed to discover how often little eyes are watching us, and how much of our lives they soak in. Grandchildren observe our every move and take to heart the words that we speak. If we say we believe and trust in the Lord, our everyday lives must be living examples of our faith. As James 1:22 reminds us, *"But be doers of the word and not hearers only."* Our actions and our words show those around us that Jesus is alive *in* us, and He delights to be invited to live in their hearts, too!

It is encouraging to know that while none of us is a perfect grandparent, we are the perfect grandparents for our grandchildren!

> *Blessed are those whose lawless deeds are forgiven, and whose sins are covered; blessed is the man to whom the LORD shall not impute sin* (Romans 4:7–8).

The Lord's design for families is so much greater than what our eyes see. He has a magnificent plan to restore families, His church, and future generations to Himself. If God's plan begins with dying, then it continues with living a life of faith and displaying his love.

Through our lives, our grandchildren can see that a living faith is about having a personal relationship with our Savior. It's about living a life that reflects the Spirit of God who abides in us. There is such love in the power of the Spirit of God that martyrs in the early church went to their deaths singing hymns of praise to Him. How wonderful it would be if that same love were to radiate from us to the next generations and lead the way to restoration in our families!

OUR PRAYER

Lord, we thank You for the gift of family. We had no idea how wonderful it would be to have grandbabies. You are truly a God of wonder. We pray that You will open the eyes of our grandchildren to see that You are alive and real! May they see You reflected in our lives. We are so aware that we fall short in this calling You have given us. We cannot leave a living legacy of faith without Your help and the power of Your Spirit. Grant us humble hearts to confess and repent when we fail. You are a good God, forgiving and kind and not willing that any should perish, but that all should come to repentance.

Thank you, Lord, for leaving us a living legacy in the person of Jesus Christ, the living Word. Grant us grace to keep pressing on toward the higher goal of the upward call in Christ Jesus.

It is in Your name we pray.

Amen.

7 • REACHING YOUNG HEARTS WITH STORIES: LEAVING A LEGACY OF WISDOM

I will open my mouth with a parable;
I will utter hidden things, things from of old—
things we have heard and known,
things our ancestors have told us.
We will not hide them from their descendants;
we will tell the next generation
the praiseworthy deeds of the LORD,
his power, and the wonders he has done.

—Psalm 78:2–4 NIV

"One of my earliest memories was snuggling with you in your bed and having you tell me stories—even when you were so tired that you fell asleep while thinking of the next thing to say."

Those were the reflections of one of our grandchildren as we reminisced recently over memories of storytelling in our family. Stories are wonderful. They have a way of reaching and captivating our hearts as few other things do. Everyone loves a good story! They are not only entertaining, but are also a wonderful way to slip inside a child's heart and deposit golden nuggets of wisdom. Embraced in the security of a grandparent's lap, children's defenses dissolve, and their hearts become open books, ready to receive whatever lessons we write on their pages. Many life lessons can be cloaked in an engaging story. Even Jesus told stories when He wanted to touch people's hearts with deeper life messages. Purposeful stories are a subtle yet powerful instrument for reaching and bonding with grandchildren.

Many of our most treasured times with our grandchildren have centered around storytelling. Opportunities to share stories can arise spontaneously as you engage in everyday activities with your grandchildren, or you can plan to set aside times for intentional storytelling. In these days when young people gravitate like magnets to electronic devices, it may take some effort and persistence to set aside time for stories and creative, imaginative activities—but it will be well worth it, for both you and your grandchildren!

Opportunities to share stories can arise spontaneously as you engage in everyday activities with your grandchildren.

If you are like us, you may find the idea of telling stories to your grandchildren to be intimidating at first. We have never considered ourselves to be naturally gifted in the art of storytelling. To be honest, we hadn't even told stories to our own children. The thought of creating meaningful stories as a tool to bond with our grandchildren was a bit overwhelming to us.

How do we create a good story? We wrestled with the challenge. *Where do we even begin?*

We were tempted to abdicate to defeat before we had even begun.

But God is a creative God, and as we sought Him for help, He began not only to give us opportunities to slip into our grandchildren's hearts with stories, but also to inspire us with captivating storylines that were fitting for each situation. Whenever the children opened windows to their hearts, it was time for Mom-Mom or Pop-Pop to be prepared to plunge in! As a result, storytelling has become one of our family's greatest pleasures and most endearing pastimes.

FOOTPRINTS FROM PAST GENERATIONS

Passing down stories from past generations is a wonderful way to give children a secure feeling of *connectedness*, to anchor their hearts to something firm and unwavering. It's been a great joy to see their little eyes alight with excitement as we tell stories of their ancestors. I might launch into a story by showing the children a photo of my grandfather and beginning, "Did you know that your great-great-grandfather Harry Leavitt missed a ferryboat ride when he was only a little older than you? He was twelve years old when he was scheduled to take a ferryboat from Portland, Maine, to Peck's Island. Grandfather arrived at the ferry ten minutes too late, and it left without him. Perhaps he felt disappointed upon discovering that he had been left behind. However, that night the boat sank, and many passengers on board died. Your great-great-grandfather's life was spared. If he had been on board that boat, where do you think *you* would be today?"

I could see their little minds mulling over that thought. Eventually one piped up, "Mom-Mom, if he had died, *you* wouldn't be here either, would you?"

Passing down stories from past generations is a wonderful way to give children a secure feeling of connectedness, to anchor their hearts to something firm and unwavering.

The door was opened to more questions and thought-provoking conversation. What a wonderful opportunity to leave footprints in their young minds of the unexpected ways of a sovereign God and His unstoppable plans for each of our lives!

Another story from past generations was one that Roger recounted to the children about the night his father nearly lost his life. He was in a convoy of ships in the Atlantic Ocean during World War II. One fateful night, the enemy torpedoed twenty-two American ships—yet his father's life was spared.

"You grandchildren were only a twinkle in the Lord's eye at the time," Roger shared, his own eyes twinkling, "but look what He did to bring you into this life and set you in our family! He protected your grandfather one dismal night in the middle of the Atlantic Ocean."

As grandparents, we have collected an arsenal of stories over the years. Children of all ages love to hear flashback stories about our lives when we were their ages.

Stories are not exclusively for young children. They are also powerful, engaging tools for reaching teenagers. With older teenagers, you can share stories as you engage in activities together. You probably have more life stories to share than you realize. After all, you were young yourself not so very long ago! While the details of your grandchildren's lives are most likely different from your own, the themes and struggles of our lives are remarkably similar. One of the most important life lessons for teenagers to learn is the importance of making responsible choices. Sometimes, we don't get a second chance to learn this lesson.

ROGER SHARES...

True stories are often greater than fiction. I remember mesmerizing our open-mouthed grandchildren with the story of the time I evaded death one cold, wintry day, as an impulsive thirteen-year-old.

Ice skating was a popular pastime for young boys during our cold New England winters. One day, a few friends and I gathered at a frozen river to skate. Skating over a flowing river is always risky, no matter how cold it is. Without testing the ice first, it's difficult to tell how thick and strong it is.

On this particular day, my buddies and I chose an idle part of the river to skate on where we knew the ice was thicker. Suddenly, without thinking, I darted away from my friends and impulsively took off skating over the flowing river. Unbeknownst to me, the river ice was treacherously thin.

Crrraaack! Crrraaack!

Frozen fingers of fractured ice created a symmetrical pattern in the ice behind me, chasing me as I skated.

Unfortunately, encroaching fear didn't shake a bit of common sense into my young head. On the brink of panic, I knew I had to make it back to the safety of the riverbank where the other boys were, but thin, fractured ice and a flowing river stood between the safety of home and where I now stood. Falling into the freezing water would have meant quick, certain death from hypothermia and drowning.

While the details of your grandchildren's lives are most likely different from your own, the themes and struggles of our lives are remarkably similar.

The only route I saw to the promise of safety was back across the dangerous, cracked ice. Controlled more by my instincts than by logic, I took off. As ice cracked beneath me, adrenaline fueled by fear kicked in! By shear will and speed, I outskated probable death, arriving panting and breathless at the safety of the riverbank.

The Lord must have sent an angel to watch over me that day, or I would not be here today to tell you this story.

As our grandchildren stared up at me with rapt attention, I slipped in a valuable life lesson: *Think before you act, so you can make wise, responsible decisions. Don't ever behave as foolishly as your Pop-Pop!*

DOTTIE SHARES...

There is something delightfully bonding about reaching the hearts of children through storytelling. When teachable moments arise, we can make the most of them by turning them into charming stories with a deeper meaning. Younger children love fictitious tales with make-believe characters and have a special fondness for animal characters and imaginary children. At a surprisingly young age, children are able to see *themselves* in animal stories.

I have often gleaned ideas for story-starters from our daughters. When they are working with one of their children on a particular character trait—such as thoughtfulness, helpfulness, or truthfulness—I create an imaginary, purposeful story with a moral lesson based on that trait, pull my grandchild onto my lap, and away we go!

As jealousy blossomed in Julie's heart, it became apparent that intervention was needed.

One of my earliest stories was created after our grandson, Jeff, was born. When Jeff came along, two-and-a-half-year-old sister, Julie, was not ready to share her little world with a brother. As jealousy blossomed in Julie's heart, it became apparent that intervention was needed. I came alongside my daughter and son-in-law to offer my support.

One afternoon before Julie's nap, I drew her onto my lap and asked her a gentle, purposeful question:

"Do you know what jealousy is, honey?" I probed.

Julie's precious heart opened up, ready for a good story, and I slipped in. As we began to rock together, I shared the following story, creating it as we went along . . .

Down in the meadow, not far from a green forest, lived a special little bunny named Fluffy. She was a much-loved bunny. She was also a spoiled little bunny. For the last two-and-a-half years, she had her mommy and daddy's attention all to herself. She liked it that way—until the day her baby brother, Ribbit, showed up.

"My life is ruined," Fluffy scowled. "I wanted a sister."

"Mom-Mom?" Julie interrupted, "*I* wanted a baby sister, too. I don't want a brother."

Now I had Julie's rapt attention. I began to probe with tender questions, preparing to transition to the moral of our story.

"Why don't you want a brother, honey? Brothers can be lots of fun."

"*No-o-o-o* they aren't, Mom-Mom. All brothers do is push trucks around and make noises."

"Well, let me continue with Fluffy's story to see how she handles her problem."

Fluffy didn't care about her little brother Ribbit's feelings. She was only thinking about herself and how much attention her mommy and daddy were giving to her brother. She felt left out and wanted her baby brother to go away. She even began to do some things like wetting her bed again and acting like a baby. She thought that she would get the same attention as Ribbit. But, it wasn't working. Her mother told her that she was a big sister now. She did not need to act like a baby again just to get attention.

Julie's precious heart opened up, ready for a good story, and I slipped in.

"I think that's terrible, Mom-Mom. I'm not going to act like a baby. I am two and a half years old. Ribbit can't help it that he is a boy. Fluffy should love her baby brother, right?"

"You know, Julie, that's exactly what Fluffy decided to do." Julie shifted on my lap and snuggled a little closer as I continued,

Mommy and Daddy assured Fluffy that they had a special love in their hearts just for her. That night, Fluffy prayed and asked the God-who-makes-bunnies to forgive her for being jealous of her new little brother.

Fluffy the bunny started being nice to her baby brother and asked to hold him more. It made her mommy and daddy very happy. In the morning, after she awoke and dressed herself like a big bunny, Fluffy went downstairs and asked her mommy how she could help today. Mommy was so happy to have a big bunny to help her!

Two years later, Fluffy's dream came true. Her mommy had a baby girl bunny.

Without waiting for me to say, "And they all lived happily ever after," Julie jumped up from my lap, ran downstairs to the cradle, leaned over, and kissed her baby brother.

"You aren't so bad, Jeffie. I kinda like you."

Storytelling was more fun than I had anticipated.

Storytelling was more fun than I had anticipated. Julie was totally entranced in the moment, hanging on to every word. On her own, she made the connection and personalized the story to her own situation.

About a month later, while out to dinner with the family, I was seated next to Julie, now three years old. Leaning toward me, Julie whispered in my ear, "Mom-Mom, can we sit by ourselves and tell stories?" Tossing back her hair she added, "Adults are so boring." I had to chuckle. We were beginning our own relationship.

As more grandchildren were added to our brood, I continued to ask the Lord to give me stories to fit various family situations. And He did. Imagine my surprise one day to discover one of our grandchildren reenacting one of my stories in front of an audience of neighborhood children! With children, we can expect they will do the unexpected!

MORE STORY IDEAS

Another story I created was for a time when two of my grandsons, Ben and Matt, needed to learn the importance of protecting their little sister. This make-believe story, called "The Big Black Cat," featured two small field mice and a black cat who was always trying to capture their little sister. The two field mice devised plans to capture the big black cat and rescue their sister. Years passed before either Ben or Matt realized the story was about *them!*

Our grandchildren never tired of hearing imaginary stories about other children who were much like themselves. Real people with real problems found their way into our stories, as well as real solutions to those problems. Perhaps the children's favorite story was "The Adventures of George and Jennifer," a fictitious story spun in my imagination that continued to entertain the children for years.

George and Jennifer were make-believe friends who embodied real-life character qualities. (They can be whatever ages you want them to be, but in our stories, they were the same ages as the grandchildren to whom I was telling the story at the time!) George and Jennifer were next-door neighbors and best friends. As the neighborhood problem-solvers, they gave me opportunities to bring valuable life lessons into their stories. On the other hand, George and Jennifer often found themselves in trouble, making them believable characters with whom our grandchildren could relate.

As more grandchildren were added to our brood, I continued to ask the Lord to give me stories to fit various family situations.

"The Adventures of George and Jennifer" featured other characters as well, each representing people in real life. There was Bully Billy and a friend named Peter, who annoyed everyone with his need to be first in everything. As the problem-solver, George became the story's peace-maker whenever competition or rivalry erupted between the boys.

For the girls, Jennifer depicted the role of neighborhood social organizer. The other girls loved her because she was fair and was careful not to exclude anyone. Jennifer's best friend was Anna, a little girl with crippled feet. Naturally, Jennifer made sure that Anna was included in the sleepovers and birthday parties—because *all* children are equally valuable in God's eyes.

Since George and Jennifer were best friends and were involved in so many adventures together, I suppose it was inevitable that our grandchildren would eventually inquire whether they got married. That opened up a whole new subject for discussion! George and Jennifer's relationship became its own special story. For several years, I managed to build great suspense by saving the answer to the question of romance as a surprise ending to the story! As each grandchild turned twelve, I revealed the surprise ending to them, making them promise not to tell their younger siblings and cousins. It became our little secret! Amazingly, none of the children gave away the secret.

Purposeful storytelling became a way for us to support our daughters and sons-in-law by reinforcing the lessons they were desiring to instill in their children.

I do not know who enjoyed storytelling more—our grandchildren or us! It was the source of much warm bonding and years of memories. As a legacy passed down, purposeful storytelling became a way for us to support our daughters and sons-in-law by reinforcing the lessons they desired to instill in their children.

Evenings passed quickly, and bedtime followed easily after a snuggly chair, a warm blanket, and a story. To be honest, it would have been temptingly convenient to turn on the television and sit the children in front of it to pass the time. However, their parents appreciated that we agreed not to do that. And so, family story time originated. Now that our grandchildren are growing up and reminiscing with us over special memories, we're so glad we invested in family story time years ago!

HINTS FOR CREATING YOUR OWN STORY-TIME LEGACY

1. Start with familiar stories that you already know. Then, adapt or enhance them to fit the situation. Make up unexpected endings, or end with a suspense-filled cliffhanger.

2. Keep it simple. Simpler stories often make better stories for children.

3. Bible stories are a wonderful source for story-time ideas.

4. Children love to act out stories. Adding in dress-up costumes makes it extra special! Look through your closet for potential costume pieces. Thrift stores and yard sales are good places to pick up inexpensive costume pieces and props with dramatic potential. *"One man's trash is a grandchild's treasure!"* Keep a costume box tucked away in your home for when the grandchildren come to visit. And don't be afraid to put on a silly outfit of your own and join in the fun!

5. Pull out a video camera and record some of the children's dramas. They will love watching "reruns" for years to come! We have also recorded some of our stories on a CD, as a legacy to be shared with our great-grandchildren.

6. A wonderful way to stimulate a child's imagination is *Build-a-Story Time*. Here's how it works: begin telling a story, then pause and say, "Pass." Your grandchild adds a few lines to the

story, then "passes" back to you. You can go back and forth, building a story between the two of you, or you can pass the story around a circle and include as many children as you like. Be prepared for totally unpredictable endings to emerge!

7. Similar to Build-a-Story is *Build-a-Picture.* This activity requires paper and a crayon or marker. To begin, start drawing a simple picture on the paper. Pass the picture to another child, who adds one thing onto the picture. Once again, you can pass the picture back and forth between the two of you, or you can include more children, each one adding something to the picture. When you decide the picture is complete, it's time for you to tell a story from the picture you and the children have created!

THOUGHTS TO PONDER

God Himself is the greatest storyteller of all and the creative inspiration for endless stories. He authored the most glorious story of all time—the gospel story! What human mind could have imagined such a story? The King of the universe left His glory in heaven and came to earth; debased Himself as a mortal man; committed no wrong, yet endured mocking, scorning, and ultimately death to save the very ones who crucified Him. No human mind could have conceived such a plan, and no human mind could have predicted the incomprehensible ending in which the Lord rose from the dead. But God not only wrote this gospel story, He also provided perfect foreshadowing of events to come through the prophets, and finally, *He lived out His entire story from beginning to end!* The best part

God Himself is the greatest storyteller of all and the creative inspiration for endless stories.

of this story will be the epilogue where Jesus returns to earth, and God establishes His kingdom on earth!

You, too, have stories to tell. They may be family stories; they may be stories from the Bible; they may be fables with deeper life messages; or they may be original stories created in your own imagination. You have many sources from which to draw stories. Tap into the wellspring of stories and experiences in your own life and begin to share them with your grandchildren. They will become a powerful and memorable legacy to leave for the next generations!

OUR PRAYER

Dear heavenly Father,

You are a creative God. You created the galaxies and the heavens. You design snowflakes. You make majestic mountains and waterfalls, and You clothe flowers and birds in beautiful splendor.

You are also a wonderful storyteller. When Jesus walked on earth, He told magnificent, poignant parables designed to open our eyes and reach our hearts with powerful lessons.

We need You to fill us with fresh, creative ideas to help us reach the young, impressionable hearts of our grandchildren. You created their hearts and minds so uniquely and wonderfully. Help us to sow wisdom into them through stories.

Thank you for being an endless source of wisdom and creativity.

In Jesus' name,

Amen.

8 · CREATING A LASTING MEMORIAL: IT'S EASIER THAN YOU THINK

When your children ask in time to come, saying, "What do these stones mean to you?" Then you shall answer them that the waters of the Jordan were cut off before the ark of the covenant of the LORD; ... And these stones shall be for a memorial to the children of Israel forever.

—Joshua 4:6–7

After forty years wandering in the wilderness, the children of Israel at last came to the land of Canaan, which the Lord had promised them. However, just outside the Promised Land, the Israelites faced an impossible obstacle: the Jordan River, which had flooded its banks, stood between the people and the Promised Land. The children of Israel needed a way to cross over the river safely. They were so close to the Lord's promised destination for them, yet an insurmountable river stood between them and the hope of entering the Promised Land. Joshua, their leader, told the Israelites that the Lord was about to perform a miracle among them. *"By this you shall know that the living God is among you"* (Joshua 3:10). When the Israelites came to the bank of the Jordan River, the Lord commanded the priests to dip their feet into the edge of the water. As soon as they did so, the waters of the Jordan River were miraculously cut off upstream and *stood still* in the place where the Israelites were waiting to cross. The priests, who were carrying the ark of the covenant of the Lord, stood firm on dry ground in the middle of the Jordan River while all the people of Israel—men, women, and children—crossed over on dry ground!

He still desires that the older generations speak to the younger ones of His wondrous works and instruct them in His ways.

Then the Lord instructed the men to take twelve stones from the Jordan River and lay the stones down on the other side of the river. These stones were to be a lasting memorial to the children, so that when they—and the generations that followed them—asked what the stones meant, they would be reminded of the great miracle the Lord had performed.

Amazingly, the Lord still works wonders for His children today. He still desires that the older generations speak to the younger ones of His wondrous works and instruct them in His ways. There is *urgency* to this message in our day. We are to be faithful to speak of the Lord's marvelous works to our children and grandchildren. This is the legacy we are to pass down: *Remember that the living God is among you and will never fail you.*

THE MEMORY BOX

No, Ella—don't! Don't open that door! Dad's thoughts shouted at his seven-year-old daughter, but there was no time for the words to escape from his mouth. What started out as the low rumble of an engine quickly intensified to a roar. Seven-year-old Ella did not see the fast-moving car approaching.

A short while earlier, Ella and her father had climbed into the family car for a drive to her grandmother's house—a trip they had made many times without incident. Excitement tinged the peaceful atmosphere as Ella and her father chatted amicably. Arriving at their destination, Ella's father began to search for a parking space. On the narrow one-way street, cars lined both sides, constricting passage even more. Finding a tiny, tight parking spot, Ella's dad inched in and parked the car. Ella, in her eagerness to see her grandmother, jumped out of her seat belt the minute the car came to a stop. Without thinking, she opened the rear car door on the street side and began to scramble out, oblivious to the speeding car barreling down the narrow road.

Hearing the roar of the approaching car's engine through the open door, Ella's father realized instantly that there was no time to get her back into the car safely and close the door. He felt helpless to prevent an impending disaster. Jerking his head around toward the back seat, he saw an incredible sight—miraculously, a strap on Ella's jumper had become caught on something behind his seat, and it pulled her back into the car, her hand still frozen in fear to the car door. A second later, the speeding car flashed by his window—so close that he could feel a stream of wind hit him as a blur of color disappeared down the road.

This is the legacy we are to pass down: Remember that the living God is among you and will never fail you.

Immediately, Ella's father jumped out of the car and gathered his daughter into his arms, which were trembling with both adrenaline and relief. Though badly frightened by the near tragedy, Ella was otherwise unhurt.

"*Dadddyyyy,*" the distraught little girl sobbed.

Her father hugged her tightly and comforted her, " You're going to be okay, Ella. God was with you. He *saved you* today."

That night, when the family gathered together for prayers of thanksgiving, Ella's father pulled out the family Memory Box. They had made the box themselves, with six pockets inside. Each family member had his or her own compartment in which to save memorable objects. The Memory Box was a family keepsake—a place to keep special tokens and remembrances of the Lord's blessings in their lives.

As Daddy reminded the family of God's kind mercy on little Ella and His ever-faithful presence, Ella placed a piece of the fabric from her jumper into her compartment in the Memory Box. Her mother had cut it from the strap that saved her. For many years after, each time the family opened the Memory Box, the piece of fabric reminded them of the time when God compassionately preserved Ella's life.

The family Memory Box contained many other memorabilia that were reminiscent of God's sovereign protection over them.

The family Memory Box contained many other memorabilia that were reminiscent of God's sovereign protection over them. A small snowboard charm along with a pair of crutches was placed in the box, reminding Ella's family of the time God healed Dad's broken leg after a snowboarding competition.

A picture of Ella's brother Donny, holding a pair of ice skates, was a memorial to the night he was rescued from a near-drowning accident while skating on thin ice.

A blue ribbon was placed in Karen's pocket after she won her first swimming meet.

Hospital baby bracelets along with baby shoes, of course, were in Mommy's pocket. The children loved to hear the stories retold that were reminiscent of each of their births.

Daddy's pocket contained a miniature figurine of a German shepherd to remind him of his time training German shepherds as patrol dogs in the Armed Forces, and of the time the dogs saved his life. His Vietnam War stories were among the children's favorites, keeping them captivated for hours.

New memorabilia are continually being added to the Memory Box. Each addition provides a special occasion for the family to gather around, share their stories, and savor the Lord's goodness. It is a wonderful practice for us all to periodically take time out of our busy lives to reminisce with our families about the meaningful and personal ways the Lord has cared for us. In fact, God's Word abounds with references to memorializing His good and merciful works for future generations.

You shall teach [these things] to your children, speaking of them when you sit in your house, when you walk by the way, when you lie down, and when you rise up (Deuteronomy 11:19).

SEIZING SMALL OPPORTUNITIES TO CREATE BIG MEMORIES

Childhood memories are powerful. They have a way of getting into our souls and hanging around for a lifetime. Although inanimate, childhood memories possess an almost lifelike ability to influence who we become as adults. They provide substance and structure throughout childhood. They become anchors that we look back on for stability during tumultuous times. As grandparents, we have an unequaled opportunity to become part of creating lasting memories for our grandchildren.

As grandparents, we have an unequaled opportunity to become part of creating lasting memories for our grandchildren.

We laugh now as we look back on some of our laborious attempts to craft memorable experiences for our children. Of all the elaborate memories we tried to create for them, we were dumbfounded to discover years later that the memory that stood out most to the girls was one of the most mundane activities of all. It was their memory of piling our whole family of five into a tiny, copper-colored 1978 Honda for the long Sunday drive to church. Poor Roger, confined in a cramped car for an hour with four women who were anything but quiet and reserved! During that hour-long drive, we sang, we laughed, and we shared stories—our voices reverberating inside the close quarters of our family car.

The key to unlocking a powerful memory is the feeling that accompanies an activity.

Creating lasting memories for grandchildren does not necessitate boarding a plane bound for Disney World or indulging in a shopping spree at the local toy store. Surprisingly, a child's most cherished memories often revolve around the simplest moments. The key to unlocking a powerful memory is the *feeling* that accompanies an activity. Happy memories are quite simply the best memories. Children are very discerning when it comes to pleasure. They soak in pleasurable feelings that accompany an activity. They long to know that they are loved and wanted; they crave having *fun*. When those pleasurable feelings accompany an activity, the memory becomes etched in a child's mind. Simply riding a bike together; catching fireflies; eating breakfast on a tablecloth spread on the back lawn; looking up pictures of helicopters and superheroes on Google Images while snuggled in a grandparent's lap; licking icing off a cake together when no one else is looking; eating dessert before dinner; camping out in the backyard, even if Grandpa snores—whatever brings your grandchildren joy is the feeling they will remember long after the day comes to an end.

MEMORY OF THE WOOD FAIRIES

The imagination of a young child is an enchanting world for grown-ups to tiptoe into. We need to be alert to the many opportunities that present themselves to do that very thing. May we never grow too old or become too busy to share in a child's world, a world that is not limited to what is logical or rational. At times, we need our grandchildren to remind us to hit the pause button on reality and the tyranny of urgent matters, and take a detour into their delightful world of make-believe.

When our grandchildren were young, one of their most memorable experiences was searching for Wood Fairies with us. Now, we know that the Land of Wood Fairies is not a real place; however, it was as real as any place could be to our grandchildren! In fact, if you have ever taken a walk through the woods, you just might have seen a few Wood Fairies yourself—or perhaps not. You see, full-grown Wood Fairies are not much bigger than large mosquitoes. They keep their distance because their luminescent wings are exceedingly delicate and can easily be damaged if touched by human hands. Though grown-ups rarely see them, these captivating creatures are plentiful in number and possess a special fondness for children. They often watch over children protectively at play. As tiny as they are, Wood Fairies are able to stealthily slip into unusual places and bless children with unexpected surprises.

May we never grow too old or become too busy to share in a child's world

Whenever we are in the woods with our grandchildren, we are always on the lookout for these elusive fairies. They have been known to hide wonderful surprises for children under bushes and rocks. To assist children in finding these surprises, Wood Fairies leave little tufts of their fairy-fuzz along the path as a guide for the children to follow. (If fairy-fuzz happens to bear an uncanny resemblance to pulled-apart cotton balls, it may be because stealthy grandparents have preceded the Wood Fairies!)

On one occasion in our family, some benevolent Wood Fairies left a very special treat of miniature chocolate bars for the children.

Joining our grandchildren in their playful world of make-believe has brought back the child in us!

A major problem soon followed: hungry chipmunks beat the children to the chocolate bars and ate all but the wrappers. After eagerly following a trail of fairy-fuzz to their anticipated surprise, the children were ever so disappointed at finding only empty wrappers. That night they gathered to compose a letter to their tiny friends:

"Dear Wood Fairies, Thank you for the treats. But please do not leave any more chocolate. Chipmunks eat it before we find it. Or maybe you could please wrap it in plastic bags next time?"

As our grandchildren grew older and figured out the truth behind the fantasy of the Wood Fairies, they were discreet enough to keep their revelations to themselves. Enthusiastically, they joined forces with us grandparents to carry on the memorable tradition. Adding their own creative touches, the older children helped to make the fairy stories even more believable for the younger children. As far as we know, none of the older grandchildren ever "spilled the beans" and spoiled the fantasy for the younger ones. The Wood Fairies are now a favorite memory that is being passed down by our grandchildren to our great-grandchildren. Who knows how many more generations will enjoy surprise encounters with the Wood Fairies?

Joining our grandchildren in their playful world of make-believe has brought back the child in us! One of our most enduring memories was creating a playhouse together.

PLAYHOUSE MEMORIES

If you've ever lamented an unsightly water heater closet in your basement, you will bless the day you converted it into a playhouse for your grandchildren! That is precisely what we did. The water heater closet in our family room soon became a well-stocked, no-frills playhouse. As we mentioned earlier, the closet boasted most everything a child's imagination could desire for a world of make-believe. Thrift stores and yard sales provided a trunk full of dress-up apparel and household items. The closet space, however, was only large enough to accommodate the little ones, so Mom-Mom had to sit at the door to join in the make-believe activities. Many elegant dinners and royal tea parties took place in that little water heater closet—with a plate of real peanut butter crackers and apple slices serving as delectable fare.

Even the boys, when they were young, enjoyed playing in the playhouse closet. Naturally, the girls took charge as the self-appointed mommies, instructing the boys that they had to be the daddies. For hours, the children entertained themselves. When the boys grew bored playing house and were ready for more action, out came the trucks. Between little boy noises, zooming trucks, and speeding cars, our family room took on a whole new dimension. We had to exercise great caution not to be run over when venturing into the family room. The girls were not deterred though. They were glad the daddies had gone to work.

One of our most enduring memories was creating a playhouse together.

The playhouse closet was a wonderful memory while it lasted, but the time came when the children outgrew it. It was time to find something bigger and better. We found just the thing: an old shed in our backyard. After a bit of clearing and cleaning, the shed was ready to become our new playhouse and the site of many new memories.

BACKYARD MEMORIES

"Help! Mom-Mom! Pop-Pop! There's a FOX in the yard! And it's after us!!" The girls shrieked and squealed in feigned fear, running as fast as their little legs could carry them.

The playhouse closet was a wonderful memory while it lasted, but the time came when the children outgrew it.

Behind the girls loped a red fox. At least, it *looked* like a red fox. But if you listened carefully, you could just barely hear muffled sounds of Dottie's laughter coming from the "fox."

"Oh Mom-Mom. You really had us fooled. We thought you were a fox!"

"I AM a fox!" Dottie chuckled in a deep fox voice. "And I am very hungry!"

A favorite pastime for our grandchildren was a make-believe game we called *Reddy the Fox*. Mom-Mom played the part of Reddy, and the grandchildren were the rabbits who lived in the playhouse shed. In this game, the children, pretending to be bunnies, set out to find an imaginary meadow to pick blueberries. From the shed at the other end of the meadow, Reddy gleefully watched as the bunnies made their way to the blueberry patch.

Stealthily, Reddy the Fox crept closer and closer, hiding behind a tree here and a bush there. Suddenly and unexpectedly, Reddy jumped out and with a big fox voice chased the bunnies. Screaming at the tops of their lungs, the bunnies dropped their buckets and ran like lightening back to the safety of their burrow in the playhouse. Soon, they ventured out cautiously to pick blueberries, and the drama repeated all over again. It made for an exciting, and exhausting, afternoon! The little "rabbits" knew that if Reddy ever caught them, they would be stew for dinner. Of course, Reddy never did. The young bunnies were too quick for old Reddy.

In addition to the old shed, our backyard hosted two sturdy trees with low-lying branches, perfect for climbing. The vivid imaginations of young boys transformed those two trees into two ships—one a pirate ship and the other an explorer's sailing vessel. High in the trees perched eager lookout scouts, scanning the horizon through paper-towel-roll telescopes. Their duty was to spot any ship that dared to pass too close. The lookout aboard the sailing vessel would cry out, "Ahoy! Approaching vessel! Trim the sails—PIRATES!" Then, aboard the pirates' ship, the cry would go out. "Hoist the flag! Prepare to go aboard, mates!"

Time slipped away as the boys acted out their fantasy war from the two trees—Pirates vs. Sailors. Out came the stick swords. First it was the pirates who climbed aboard the sailors' tree-ship—then vice-versa. The play drama continued until either the pirates nabbed the booty, or the sailors saved the gold. The outcome was different each time the boys played. Lunch was always late on days when there was a pirate war to win.

On days when we took the grandchildren wading in the creek, they were up at the crack of dawn. Jumping into bed with us, they pulled the covers off, prodding us impatiently, "It's time to go to the creek, Mom-Mom and Pop-Pop!" We passed around tickles and laughter and soon were ready for our big adventure.

> **Time slipped away as the boys acted out their fantasy war from the two trees— Pirates vs. Sailors.**

Wading in the creek was a big event. The children were usually far too excited to eat much breakfast, so we packed snacks into a backpack. Pants were rolled up and into the water we went, pretending we were pioneers looking for our next meal. Spotting a school of minnows, Pop-Pop teased the children, "You better watch out or the minnows will bite your toes!"

"No, Pop-Pop! Don't scare us like that!" the girls pleaded squeamishly at the thought of their toes being nibbled by fish.

Being the rugged "men" that they were, the boys ignored the girl-talk and kept on trudging through the creek. Quietly the girls joined them, and we all followed the school of minnows till they disappeared under a bridge. It was time to turn around and go home. With sneakers full of sand and soaking wet clothes, it had been another day to remember. As a special Grandma and Grandpa treat, we topped off creek memories with hot chocolate and cookies *before* lunch!

As a special Grandma and Grandpa treat, we topped off creek memories with hot chocolate and cookies before lunch!

Another special outdoor memory we created with our grandchildren was the construction of an Indian tepee. On a hill overlooking the creek near our home, we took the older grandchildren into the woods to build a tepee. We scavenged the area in search of sizable, dead tree branches, which we stood firmly together against a tree. It made a perfect tepee. The children gathered smaller branches on the ground to fill in the gaps. The tepee was spacious enough for all of us to fit inside for a picnic. What fun we had pretending that we were early pioneers!

For many years, every time the children came to visit, they wanted to see if the tepee was still standing. Even the four younger grandchildren, who lived three hours away, looked forward to visiting the tepee whenever they stayed with us. It became a very special memory for all the grandchildren. With only a few repairs, our tepee survived for quite a few years before it finally deteriorated.

We were certainly blessed to have a wooded area nearby. However, if you don't, even small clumps of trees or bushes in residential neighborhoods can offer great creative potential. By cutting away a few inside branches, you can create a secret hideout or fort, perfect for special times with Grandma and Grandpa! There are plenty of ways to create a makeshift tepee using the children's imaginations. Home improvement stores offer a variety of sturdy tarps; camping departments in discount stores do, also. A tarp can be tied to a few stakes or sticks embedded in the ground or suspended between trees. A picnic basket can be taken virtually anywhere—and will turn any spot into a memorable outdoor homestead. Indians ate corn—so fill a picnic basket with popcorn and red or blue corn chips. The children can go by Indian names for the afternoon—like "Chief Love To Eat Tree Bark!" Of course, anyone entering the frontier hideout must give the secret password!

Our converted playhouse shed and the tepee lasted for nearly ten years. It was a sad day when we moved away, but we took with us in our hearts many joy-filled memories.

TRAVELING DOWN MEMORY LANE WITH GRANDCHILDREN

In our family, many lasting memories with our grandchildren have been built around family photo albums. Full of family history, photo albums have the magical ability to transport us back in time, serving as springboards to endless bonding conversations. Most intrigued by the old black-and-white photos, the children were often off and chattering.

A picnic basket can be taken virtually anywhere—and will turn any spot into a memorable outdoor homestead.

"Who are the old man and woman dressed in those funny clothes?" the children asked, as we nestled together on the couch.

"Your great-great-grandmother Mary and your great-great-grandfather Harry."

"Mary and Harry? Hey, they rhymed!" the children giggled, going off on an unexpected tangent.

"They were married when they were only eighteen years old. They look pretty young, don't they? See that horse and buggy? That's what Mary and Harry rode around in when they were courting."

"That must have been fun to have a horse! But didn't they get cold riding in that buggy in the winter? What's courting?"

"Courting is what young ladies and fellows used to do when they were thinking about getting married. They got to know one another under the watchful eyes of their parents."

"Yep. Parents sure like to watch stuff. Did people have electricity in their houses back then?"

Full of family history, photo albums have the magical ability to transport us back in time, serving as springboards to endless bonding conversations.

"No—no electricity. No running water either."

"That's hard to imagine. It sounds like *The Little House on the Prairie*."

"It was in some ways. By the turn of the twentieth century, most people had running water and electricity, but outhouses were still in use." *Outhouses.* Now *that's* a funny concept to try to describe to children of the twenty-first century!

As the children flipped through album pages of the past, pictures of us began to pique their interest and curiosity.

"Grandma and Grandpa, tell us about when you were little. Did you have an outhouse, too?"

"No, we didn't have an outhouse. By the time we were married, there was indoor plumbing." We could tell the children were a bit disappointed by that answer. "We did have a black-and-white television, though, and the screen was only ten inches wide."

"Black-and-white TV? *Ten inches?*" The children exchanged incredulous looks between them. "How could you see anything? How many channels did you have?"

"We only had three channels."

"Only *three* channels? Wasn't that boring?"

"Oh honey, it wasn't boring. It was all we knew. Just the thought of watching a movie in our own house was amazing to us. Not many people owned a television at first because they were so expensive. In fact, an older couple who lived next door were the first in the neighborhood to own a television. They loved children, so every afternoon at five o'clock, they invited the neighborhood kids in to watch the *The Howdy Doody Show* and enjoy home-baked treats."

We have spent many happy hours traveling down Memory Lane with only our grandchildren and a family photo album.

As the children flipped through album pages of the past, pictures of us began to pique their interest and curiosity.

CREATING LONG-DISTANCE MEMORIES

"Our grandchildren live far away. How can we build meaningful memories with them?"

Fear not! You now live in the twenty-first century! Staying connected has never been easier. Grandchildren of any age appreciate quick text messages or FaceTime or Skype from someone who cares and is thinking of them enough to reach out. You can simply send quick texts throughout the day:

"Just wanted you to know I'm thinking of you."

"Just wondering how your day is going?"

"Just letting you know somebody loves you."

An unexpected "XOXO" or a picture of something you know your grandchild will appreciate sends a message of love loud and clear!

A few generational hints: keep texts short. Learn a few current "texting-speak" shortcuts, such as emoticons (emojis). Let your grandchildren teach you what you don't already know. Surprise them with what you learn on your own by Googling "text and chat acronyms." Most important of all, do not take it personally if a grandchild does not respond to a text message. It's not personal. It's a generational thing. Young people today just don't respond to every text message. It's enough to know that you reached out and shared a word of love or encouragement. That will mean something to them. Be careful to avoid phrases like, "Did you get my last text? Why didn't you respond? I thought you must deathly sick or lying crippled in a hospital bed." Your young people will appreciate you even more if you don't require a response from them. They will reciprocate with appreciation and devotion in their own time.

Grandchildren of any age appreciate quick text messages or FaceTime or Skype from someone who cares and is thinking of them enough to reach out.

If you have a strong relationship with your grandchildren, *rejoice!* If your relationship is shaky or strained, be encouraged. It's never too late to begin building new bridges and praying that your overtures of love and care will fall on receptive hearts. The love of God is *irresistible.* The Lord is a God who restores the years that the locust has eaten (Joel 2:25).

THOUGHTS TO PONDER

We need to be mindful to acknowledge that myriad life situations have led to painful, broken families for so many of us. Even the mere mention of past experiences can resurrect painful memories. Not all recollections are worthy of remembering. To be honest, most of us have memories we wish we could forget. Grandparenting can be complicated in these situations. Yet, beauty can still be restored from ashes. If we allow families to fall apart, we will lose one of the Lord's greatest blessings. Reaching out and embracing grandchildren in the midst of these situations, while showing them grace and understanding, can be just the thing to bring healing to painful situations or broken relationships over time. Restoring and strengthening families is a treasure worth fighting for!

We can neither escape the past nor change what is past—but we do not have to *dwell* there. There *is* hope. Christ's unconditional love and forgiveness release a healing balm into our souls and into our grandchildren's lives, if they are affected. The love and forgiveness of our Savior have the power to set us free from past painful memories and give us a new hope and a future.

2 Corinthians 5:17 ESV declares, *"Therefore, if anyone is in Christ, he is a new creation. The old has passed away; behold the new has come."* Painful memories no longer have the power to consume us or control us. Jesus arose from the grave to declare victory over sin once and for all, even the sin that others may have committed against us. A painful memory may still linger, but the emotional sting can be washed away through the cleansing blood of Jesus.

> **Restoring and strengthening families is a treasure worth fighting for!**

Seizing opportunities to create memories, both big and small, with grandchildren at any age may seem simplistic, but we can't overlook the tremendous value of doing so. Through memorable moments with grandchildren, we are building bridges into their lives. We are strengthening our relationships with them so that when the trials of life come upon them, they will know they have pillars of strength and open arms to turn to. All it takes is willingness on our part to invest our time into them and sow seeds of wisdom. We can partner with parents to lead our grandchildren to the love and forgiveness of God, and to guide them along the road of wisdom.

Let us live lives worthy of emulating. The legacy of a godly life, lived faithfully, speaks volumes to a child.

If we, as grandparents, fail to pick up the baton and pass it to the next generation, the world will invariably step in and intercept it. The clamoring voices and influences of the world will not hesitate to speak into the impressionable ears of our young people. It is our duty, our privilege, and our joy to be the voices that speak loudest of all into their hearts!

Through memorable moments with grandchildren, we are building bridges into their lives.

It is time to enjoy creating your own lasting memorials—and it's simpler than you think!

OUR PRAYER

Dear heavenly Father,

Your love for Your children and our grandchildren is more than we can imagine. Their futures are in Your capable, sovereign hands. May we witness their salvations imminently—to Your glory and praise.

Lord, we need Your help to live lives daily that reflect Your humility and love, lives that are a testimony to Your Spirit who abides in us. May we be pillars of strength in our families, able to show kindness, mercy, and love, even if it is not always reciprocated. May we be longsuffering and filled with joy. May You fill us with Your creative Spirit to inspire us with ideas for creating enduring memories for our grandchildren.

Thank you for Your awesome presence and Your sustaining love. You are truly Immanuel—God with us!

In Your name we pray, Lord Jesus Christ.

Amen.

1. Roger makes his move!
Wedding day, 1958

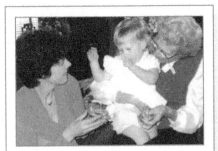

2. The two grandmas, Ruth & Dottie,
sharing their first granddaughter

3. The tradition continues—
grandbaby's first bath

4. Oldest & youngest granddaughters

5. Family identity: creating a
wall of portraits

6. "The Four Littles"

7. *Leading the search for Wood Fairy fluff*

8. *We found the Fairy's hideout!*

9. *Protecting the homestead from pirate attacks*

10. *Reaching young hearts with stories*

11. *Using small opportunities to create lasting memories*

12. *Another story for the girls*

FROM OUR SCRAPBOOK

13. Special time with Mom-Mom

14. The beauty of a shared experience

15. Sewing lessons

16. Three little soldiers

17. The grandkids love when
Roger reads to them.

18. The heart of family traditions: the
annual Christmas pageant

19. *A powwow in the backyard tepee*

20. *Mom-Mom teaching manners with "Mumble Bumble"*

21. *Kim & Warren's family*

22. *Lisa & Doug's family*

23. *Robin & Mike's family*

24. *Living and leading as a patriarch: four generations of the Roger R. Small family*

FAMILY MEMBERS BY PHOTO (LEFT TO RIGHT)

1. Roger & Dottie Small

2. Dottie, Julie, Ruth

3. Dottie, Stephen

4. Julie, Lianna

5. Wall of photos

6. Stephen, Lianna, Melanie, Tim

7. Julie, Kristie, Amy, Grant, Kevin

8. Kristie, Amy

9. Kristie, Matthew, Ben

10. Roger, Grant, Kevin

11. Amy, Dottie

12. Kristie, Dottie

13. Andy, Dottie

14. Doug, Mike, Robin, Roger, Warren, Julie, Jeff, Ben, Matt, Julie, Kristie

15. Dottie, Melanie

16. Timothy, Grant, Kevin

17. Ben, Jeff, Roger, Julie, Matthew

18. Andy, Melanie, Grant, Kevin, Kristie, Tim, Amy, Lianna

19. Stephen, Melanie

20. Dottie

21. Kim & Warren's family

22. Lisa & Doug's family

23. Robin & Mike's family

24. Living and leading as a patriarch: four generations of the Roger R. Small family

9 • ENTERING A TEENAGER'S WORLD

Hear, my son, and receive my sayings,
And the years of your life will be many.
I have taught you in the way of wisdom;
I have led you in right paths.
When you walk, your steps will not be hindered,
And when you run, you will not stumble.
Take firm hold of instruction, do not let go;
Keep her, for she is your life.

—Proverbs 4:10–13

Just when we thought we had learned the secrets to reaching the hearts of our grandchildren, a whole new species of humanity crept into our family seemingly overnight, catching us unaware—teenagers!

Teenagers. *Intimidating,* you may be thinking. *Complex. Turbulent.* Tell anyone you have teenagers in the house, and you often elicit reactions ranging from a sympathetic silence, to an *I-feel-sorry-for-you* expression, to a despairing *Will I ever get through this season?* Some folks dread the onset of the teenage years and kick into survival mode in the midst of them. Some assume that teenage years are inevitably characterized by conflicts, with childrearing being reduced to a daily challenge to endure and minimize those inescapable conflicts. Many a competent parent has been brought to his or her knees in prayer during this pivotal season of a child's life. If anyone needs encouragement, it is the parents. These can be trying years. But take heart! The teenage years can also be the best years of a young person's life. They present grandparents many priceless opportunities to build relationships and sow seeds of wisdom into precious young hearts.

The teen years are a time when young people come into their own, developing their own unique persona apart from Mom and Dad. Sure, they may try out a few strange hats along the way as they try to find a good fit, but didn't we at that age?

It takes patience to listen, not only to a teenager's words, but also to what their hearts are saying between the lines.

These are the years God designed for young people to begin to individuate and develop their own identities, opinions, and convictions. Teenagers are not necessarily rebelling against their upbringing; rather, they have a need to own matters for themselves. These are the years in which teenagers stretch and beat their fledgling wings, getting ready for independent flight. As the author of Proverbs predicted so wisely, some of their choices are foolish ones. But that has been the case for millennia, in every culture. Of all seasons in life, *this* is the one in which young people need the wisdom of generations that have gone before them. As grandparents, the onset of the teen years offers us a whole new array of opportunities.

Teenagers are really quite simple creatures. They have the same basic needs as the rest of us: the need to feel that they belong, that they are special and valued. Basically, teens want someone to value them enough to listen to them and affirm them. It takes patience to listen, not only to a teenager's words, but also to what their hearts are saying between the lines. Sometimes that is all they want us to do—simply listen to them, attentively and patiently, and accept them for who God

made them to be. They are not yet "little adults"; they are often insecure and struggling to find their way. What they need are strong, godly
role models, a dose of confidence, and the security of knowing they are
loved and valued. As a complement to parents, *grandparents* are the
ideal candidates for the job!

Relationships with teenage grandchildren can be very simple but
sincere. Genuine, caring sincerity is in short supply in many venues of
life. To encounter this at home is one of the most meaningful family
identities we can create.

Our grandson Matt, now twenty-nine years old, recently shared
with us in a letter some memories of his teenage years:

> *One very distinct memory I have is reading the Bible with Mom-*
> *Mom one night before bed. I was probably about eight years old at*
> *the time. We were reading through the*
> *crucifixion story, and the way Mom-*
> *Mom explained it made it feel so real*
> *that I wanted to keep reading it over*
> *and over again. She read Bible stories*
> *with real conviction, and she had a*
> *way of making stories come to life. I*
> *remember thinking at that young age,*
> *"If it's that real for Mom-Mom, then*
> *it has to be real!"*

**Sometimes that is
all they want us to
do—simply listen to
them, attentively and
patiently, and accept
them for who God
made them to be.**

> *A memory that stands out with Pop-Pop is that he always made*
> *me feel comfortable talking to him about anything. I never felt like*
> *he was going to judge me. I always felt that he took me seriously.*
> *As a teenager, that meant something to me as I was trying to figure*
> *things out for myself. Whether it was catching up at family gather-*
> *ings or driving in the car together, I knew he was always willing to*
> *listen and would give me a wise response.*

For a time, Matt followed in the footsteps of Roger's living legacy. Working together in the same office with Roger, Matt not only left faithful footprints for his own three children, but he and Roger created a legacy together—grandfather and grandson.

For us, in many ways, the teenage years were the season in which we reaped the fruit of our early years of telling stories and playing together. In other ways, our relationships with our young adult grandchildren changed markedly. With teenagers, building memories became more about building *relationships*—relationships that gave us a platform from which to speak into their lives when they asked.

> **The teenage years were the season in which we reaped the fruit of our early years of telling stories and playing together.**

We learned to resist the temptation to correct everything our teenagers said or did, or to give unsolicited advice. We could not be constantly critiquing and rearranging their worlds. Instead, we thought of ourselves as their *sounding boards*. We often were another set of listening ears, asking strategic questions where appropriate and listening far more than we spoke. We treated their ideas and feelings as treasures of great worth with which they entrusted us. More often than not, as young adults, our grandchildren solved their own problems as we did little more than listen to them.

In the end, wherever our conversations took us, we concluded by encouraging our teens to talk to their parents if they had not already done so. We felt we needed to be respectful of their parents' role and careful not to interfere with their advice. We certainly did not want to jeopardize our relationships with our daughters and sons-in-law in the process.

Our granddaughter Julie, now thirty years old, wrote the following email to us recently:

You created a climate where I was comfortable talking to you about real things in my life—from 3-year-old-being-scared kind of things, to 6-year-old-losing-my-favorite-doll kind of things, to 9-year-old-feeling-like-I-had-no-friends kind of things. Whatever my season in life has been, you have shared it with me. You never, ever usurped the role of my parents, even when I really wanted you to! You always supported them. You also made me feel very safe talking to you. I knew that anything I said to you, you would take seriously—and that didn't start when I was 30 years old; that started when I was 3 years old.

For us, entering into a teenager's world often meant entering into their activities—sometimes just doing what *they* were doing alongside them. For example, Dottie enjoyed playing basketball with the grandsons. However, admittedly, sometimes she was no match for the boys! There came a time when they were just too good to play against ol' Mom-Mom! At that point, Dottie became their enthusiastic cheerleader from the sidelines.

A word of encouragement may be helpful at this point: do not ever feel inadequate if you cannot keep up with the energy and pace of grandchildren. Reality says that age inexorably takes its toll on all of us. Nevertheless, your grandchildren will appreciate the effort you make to enter into their worlds, however you choose to show it. So what if we have to stretch and warm-up for twenty minutes before the grandkids come to visit? It will be worth it!

MALE BONDING

ROGER SHARES...

Living among so many of the female gender has given me countless opportunities to observe the stark contrast between boys and girls! Oh how different God has made males and females! I had to learn a whole new language, it seems. With girls one has to learn to make eye contact when holding conversations with them. At the risk of overgeneralizing, girls typically don't want you to multi-task—girls want your undivided attention.

While a granddaughter may say, "Please put your newspaper down and *talk* to me," grandsons often prefer to talk while doing activities together. Paradoxically, sitting a teenage boy down for a meaningful talk may produce little more than grunts, silence, or frustration. Meaningful male conversation is more often forged while working on a car or doing a project together. Some men I know take their teenagers to favorite "guy-type" activities, such as football games, as a means of reaching them. It becomes easier to slip strategic words of wisdom into the conversation while sharing activities together: "You know you really shouldn't talk to your mother the way I heard you the other day. What was behind that?"

> **Meaningful male conversation is more often forged while working on a car or doing a project together.**

In general, boys don't like to feel confronted—so take a hike together while you talk along the way. Often, I just listen while my grandsons do the talking, and I use the subjects they bring up as catalysts for our conversations. At other times, I inquire of my sons-in-law. They sometimes have particular issues they want me to bring up for discussion with their sons.

Being the grandfather of teenagers presents many wonderful opportunities! As we mellow with age, we can often slip in through the back door of a teenager's heart and sow lasting seeds of mutual respect and friendship.

DANGER! THE ULTIMATE MALE BONDING EXPERIENCE

It was August on Mount Washington. We had taken our daughters and some of their neighborhood friends with us on our annual mountain-climbing excursion. Full of impetuous youthful energy—and a touch of foolishness—the boys in the group charged ahead. Anyone who has been around teenage boys knows how impulsive they can be. They also operate under the illusion that they are invincible.

For the first time that summer, in Tuckerman's Ravine, there was a snow cave. This was a potentially dangerous area into which streams had flowed and created a cave beneath the surface of the snow. When unseen by climbers and hikers, snow caves can be extremely dangerous. They collapse easily, especially in the warmer summer months, smothering anyone trapped inside.

Because of the danger, rangers had taped off the area surrounding the entrance to the cave. But boys will be boys. The boys with me ran ahead and jumped over the yellow warning tape, leaping into the snow cave thinking it was great fun. Instinctively I yelled at the boys, *"Get OUT of there!"* Hearing my loud warning, a stranger nearby

There is no doubt that our close brush with disaster left an endearing bond between us!

tapped me on the shoulder and admonished, "Don't you realize *your voice* is enough to collapse that cave?" Sheepishly, I could only thank the Lord for assigning extra angels to watch over my charges that day. From that day forward, I learned to curb my hasty impulses that could have led to disaster.

Today, I cringe as I recollect the memory, but our family also laughs about it in hindsight. There is no doubt that our close brush with disaster left an endearing bond between us!

Investing in the lives of grandchildren reaps priceless treasure. Yes, we have made many mistakes, and yes, there are things we would have done differently given the opportunity. But with God's help, we have done the best we could with the knowledge and grace we had at the time. Over the years the Lord has helped us build trust in our grandchildren's eyes. He has taught us the difference between *prying* and being *available* with a listening ear when a teenager is ready to open the window to his or her heart. He has enabled us to see into their young hearts with His compassion and understanding.

> **Investing in the lives of grandchildren reaps priceless treasure.**

As our grandchildren grow older, our relationships have grown closer. There are few things more rewarding for us than a teenage grandchild stopping by spontaneously for a chat. Of course, with teenagers, talking is typically facilitated by eating! We learned to be prepared to keep their bottomless stomachs filled! Their impromptu visits provide us with opportunities to inquire about their spiritual lives, their college decisions, their work plans, their future spouses, and any other topics on their minds. We often use these times to inquire how we can pray for them. As grandparents, it is a great blessing when they make time for us in their busy lives.

We have clearly become more mellow as we have aged. We are probably in good company with countless others when we admit that we have allowed our grandchildren to do things that we did not let our own children do. When confronted by this inconsistency, our only defense can be: *That* is a privilege that comes with the territory of grandparenting!

THOUGHTS TO PONDER

Perhaps you were not raised this way. Perhaps you don't know where to begin to create a legacy that reaches the hearts of your teenage grandchildren. Be encouraged that you are not alone. Many of us were raised by parents who believed that providing for children's physical needs was the sole role of parents—much like the sparrows in our nest. The concept of listening to children, discerning what their hearts are trying to say between the lines, and affirming their immeasurable worth is a relatively new concept in human societies and cultures.

You will probably not do the same things *we* did as grandparents. We are different people with unique gifts and talents. It is exciting to recognize that *you* are the grandparents that the Lord has chosen *intentionally* for your grandchildren. You will create your own unique ways of relating to your teenagers. Your ways will spring from who you are and the gifts and strengths you bring to the family party.

In conclusion, the Lord knew that we would need help navigating uncharted waters and challenging territory in this life. That is why He left us a Helper—the Holy Spirit. *"And I will pray the Father, and He will give you another Helper, that He may abide with you forever—the Spirit of truth"* (John 14:16–17). Ask the Lord freely for wisdom whenever you need it. He will answer. You'll see! *"If any of you lacks wisdom, let him ask of God, who gives to all liberally and without reproach, and it will be given to him"* (James 1:5).

> **The Lord knew that we would need help navigating uncharted waters and challenging territory in this life.**

OUR PRAYER

Dear heavenly Father,

Thank you for Your faithfulness in helping us to navigate the turbulent teenage years. The days we rode the emotional roller coaster with our own children, You took hold of us, steadying us. And now we turn to You again and ask You to come alongside our children and their spouses as they raise our teenage grandchildren.

The world is a very different place from the one in which we raised our children. It seems that many are doing what they deem right in their own eyes. It is much like the days of the Judges. We pray, Father, that You will enable us to lead our grandchildren to the saving knowledge that Your way is far better than any of the counterfeit pleasures this world has to offer them. Without You, there is no hope for their future.

As for us, we now play a different role, in a different season. The days we have with our grandchildren are precious and short, passing by so quickly before our young people fly from the nest independently. Help us to make each day count.

Lord, give us wisdom and courage to lead them well, patience to hear what their hearts are saying between the lines, mercy to keep short accounts, and grace to model the gospel before their eyes.

We trust You with our grandchildren's futures. Your plans for them were formed long ago in perfect faithfulness, and You will go before them into the future, ushering them in after You.

We come to You in the name of our perfect Savior, Jesus.

Amen.

10 • THE HEART OF FAMILY TRADITIONS

For since the creation of the world God's invisible qualities—his eternal power and divine nature—have been clearly seen, being understood from what has been made.

—Romans 1:20 NIV

Great is the LORD and most worthy of praise;
his greatness no one can fathom.
One generation commends your works to another;
they tell of your mighty acts.
They speak of the glorious splendor of your majesty—
and I will meditate on your wonderful works.

—Psalm 145:3–5 NIV

New Hampshire's Mount Washington is a majestic wonder, an impressive testimony of God's awesome creation. Soaring 6,288 feet above the earth, Mount Washington is the highest peak in the northeastern United States.

The quest to climb Mount Washington started with Roger. Soon, our daughters joined him. In an old red van with all but the driver's seat removed, our young, energetic girls rounded up a group of their neighborhood friends—with the promise of the adventure of a lifetime! We packed like sardines into a van designed to hold fourteen.

The young socialites conversed happily together on the floor of the van as Roger drove to the base of the mountain. Together, we tackled and conquered the heights of Mount Washington!

Our original group of climbers grew as each of our girls married, and their husbands and children joined us. Soon, this challenging expedition became an annual family tradition. Old memories were recalled with fondness, and new memories were added with each successive year.

It was now August, an entire generation later, and the sun was beckoning to us from a clear, inviting sky. It was the day we had planned to respond to nature's invitation to ascend a mile into the sky. With us were our grandchildren, ages ten and older, our sons-in-law, and our daughters. This was the onset of what would become our most memorable family tradition. Starting at Pinkham Notch Ranger Station, our goal was to hike the rugged Tuckerman Ravine Trail of Mount Washington. Our physical limits were about to be put to the test. Exhilarating excitement collided with a foreboding sense of uncertainty: *What had we gotten ourselves into?* Foremost in our minds loomed the sobering responsibility for the safety of our grandchildren. Thankfully, we had a posse of parents with us to help with supervision, yet our thoughts could not escape the protective mindset, "once a parent, always a parent." We felt the burden of responsibility heavily upon our shoulders.

Eager yet apprehensive about the rigors of a mountain climb, we set out.

Like young colts out of the gate, the younger grandchildren burst ahead along the trail, not pausing to catch their breath until they reached the first waterfall. It was futile to try to harness their energy and keep them from running ahead. By the time we caught up with them, they had run through a quiet forest, crossed a thrashing brook, and were waiting for us older folks with their boots already off, dipping their feet in a cool mountain stream. Little did they know that they would need to pace themselves and reserve their energy for the rugged ascent to the summit.

After pausing to dry small feet and retrieve hiking boots, the children were antsy to begin the long climb up Mount Washington.

As we climbed, we could see the trees becoming more scattered. We were approaching the timberline, the boundary above which trees could no longer grow due to the harshness of the weather. Yet there we were. Our trail began to climb parallel to a mountain stream that flowed swiftly downhill toward the canyon. At last, we reached the ranger's cabin and with it, a chance for a brief rest before tackling the second half of our climb.

Surrounded on three sides by sheer rock walls, the Tuckerman Ravine enveloped us with the sensation of being in the Alps. Even in August, snow could be seen in the canyon. Looking ahead, we could see the headwall, a vertical cliff with stone steps cut into one side for climbing and a sheer drop on the other side. As we pressed on, the air gradually grew thinner, making it more difficult for us to breathe. Even the resilient lungs of the children were straining.

Foremost in our minds loomed the sobering responsibility for the safety of our grandchildren.

The precipitous walls of the ravine soon gave way to a vertical cliff. We had reached the headwall. We pressed on, up the twenty-story-high rock "steps." Mount Washington, infamous for its high winds and erratic weather, was true to its reputation that day. Upon reaching the top of the headwall, the mountain greeted us with whipping winds and a biting chill. The younger grandchildren drew close to us as we clung to the trail together. It was time to don warm sweaters, jackets, and hats for the final ascent. Pausing to look around, the view was breathtaking. We could see for miles. This was the final push to the summit—and new challenges that awaited us.

Suddenly, the trail vanished. In its place lay a precarious half-mile stretch of large boulders, requiring the agility of a mountain goat to jump from one stone to the next. This was the place known as *The Cone*. The children clambered over the boulders with energy fueled by a brief second wind. Their enthusiasm spurred us on as Roger and I plodded up the rear, our endurance waning but our spirits soaring. We were most grateful to see yellow paint at the top of the rock formations marking the trail. Without the paint to guide us, we would have lost the trail when the clouds closed in.

We had shared a genuine challenge of endurance together with our grandchildren—and we had conquered it together!

Urged on by the distant steam whistle of the Cog Railway as it left the summit station above us, we were now in sight of our goal. At last, exhausted but exhilarated, we sat perched victoriously atop Mount Washington, taking in the breathtaking view around us and marveling at the spectacular display of God's beauty.

After trail snacks and a brief rest, it was time for our descent. The return hike down the mountain, though not as breathless as the ascent, proved every bit as rugged and challenging. Our legs begged for mercy as our muscles tensed with each step, straining to hold us back and control our descent. What a relief it was to make it back to our van before nightfall. Piling into the van for the trek back to camp, we were overwhelmed with a collective sense of elated exhaustion. We had shared a genuine challenge of endurance together with our grandchildren—and we had conquered it together! What a memory. The young mountain climbers were proud to claim an enviable achievement in their lives.

Reflecting later on the day's adventure, Roger mused humorously, "When you climb Mount Washington, it's like you're climbing your *grandfather*. The mountain is majestic and stark. It's immovable. Yet it's approachable. And you can climb all over it!"

Reflecting more deeply on our experience, mountain climbing has become part of the intangible legacy we are passing down to our grandchildren. Mountains embody the multi-faceted contrasts of the Lord's magnificent character. On one hand, Mount Washington, in the eastern U.S., is a picture of the approachable, welcoming nature of God for those who are His children. On the other hand, the barely accessible peaks of the Rocky Mountains, out west, allude to the majestic and holy nature of God.

We all agreed that climbing Mount Washington with our grandchildren, children, and spouses was an unforgettable experience—an experience we could hardly wait to repeat. And thus, a family tradition was born.

Mountains embody the multi-faceted contrasts of the Lord's magnificent character.

As the years passed, and our grandchildren grew older, the leadership of this tradition began to pass from Roger to our sons-in-law. Every other year, they planned a challenging outdoor adventure for the men of the family. Our grandsons, beginning at thirteen years of age, could join the men in hiking the Appalachian Trail, whitewater canoeing on the Delaware River, or hiking mountains in the West. Excursions included overnight stays on the trail or riverbank. Not content with mediocre challenges, the men have graduated to progressively greater adventures. A few years ago, they conquered Glacier National Park together! Although Roger is still able to participate with the young guys, he groans that the mountains seem to grow higher with each passing year, and chairlifts are becoming a more welcome sight!

Perhaps you may be thinking, "Well, that sounds like a nice tradition for your family, but we don't happen to have a mountain to climb in our neighborhood."

Don't let the topography of your backyard stop you from becoming an adventurous trailblazer with your grandchildren! There are myriad ways to create rustic traditions with your family—limited only by your imagination! Parks, hiking trails, and creeks can be found where you least expect them. Better yet, huddle up with your Internet–savvy grandchildren and hunt together for inviting destinations to explore. Even a tent pitched in the backyard with a makeshift fire pit will satisfy a child's longing to experience natural creation. Grab some flashlights, sleeping bags, marshmallows, and an extra-large can of bug repellent—and start your own outdoor slumber party tradition. Children love falling asleep to the euphonic sounds of nature and the sight of a starry sky. It's okay if Grandma and Grandpa have to make a few trips indoors to use the bathroom facilities during the night—it will be worth it! And don't worry if it rains—stay out anyway. Some of the greatest memories are forged around *shared suffering!* You will hear the stories embellished year after year as your grandchildren reminisce over your perilous backyard adventures: "Grandpa, do you remember the time when we...?!"

Don't let the topography of your backyard stop you from becoming an adventurous trailblazer with your grandchildren.

If the alluring outdoors is not quite your thing, lasting memories can be forged in your own living room instead. A sheet pitched over the dining room table becomes a mysterious cave, and blankets stretched between couches can turn your living room into a cozy, inviting tent.

Bring a board game, a flashlight, and of course, snacks, and crawl inside with your grandchildren. Permitting them to sleep all night in their homemade lodging will be a memorable, bonding treat for all of you!

TRADITIONS ARE THE SUPER GLUE

Traditions are like glue—they bond a family together. Traditions create a backbone of stability, security, and comfort for family members. The degree to which family values impact each generation is the degree to which the glue that cements families together is strong. Often, family traditions are the strongest and most endearing "glue" of childhood memories. Even the simplest traditions give family members a vital, valuable sense of identity—as in our family's long, cramped Sunday drives to church. Traditions have a way of giving children and teenagers a sense of security. How often, when a child or grandchild brings a "special friend" or date home, do they gravitate to the family photo albums as if to say, *"This* is who we are as a family. *This* is our identity."

> **Traditions create a backbone of stability, security, and comfort for family members.**

ROGER SHARES...

By continuing family traditions, we bind our children and grandchildren to our family's past and help to prepare them for the future. Repeated year after year, traditions mark the passage of time and provide an element of predictability in an unpredictable world. Creating family traditions, and passing them down to our grandchildren, is an important part of keeping our families' bonds strong. What wonderful, healing opportunities traditions have provided in our family—opportunities to reclaim the memories and family identity that were lost to me many years ago.

BIRTHDAY BONDING–REACHING YOUNG HEARTS THROUGH SPECIAL ACTIVITIES

Traditions create a family identity that is as unique and special as each individual family. One of our family's favorite traditions is something we call *Birthday Bonding*. Each year for their birthdays, the grandchildren come over for a day of special-time activities with Mom-Mom and Pop-Pop, ending with an overnight stay. The day is theirs, for a special activity of their choice. (If their parents had other plans for their birthdays, we felt it was our place to work around *their* plans. The goal was to have a special day in honor of the child's birthday, so we tried to schedule Birthday Bonding days as close to the actual birth dates as schedules permitted.)

For his special birthday activity, four-year-old Jeff wanted to go on a fox hunt with us. Sporting a backpack with a plastic baseball bat sticking out, grandson, Pop-Pop, and Mom-Mom headed for the woods, determined to catch a fox. With video camera in hand, Roger brought up the rear. Jeff, chatting all the way, was focused on capturing his fox. Somehow the fox always eluded him. But an empty backpack never discouraged Jeff. There was always another year and another fox to be caught.

For Kristie's Birthday Bonding activity, she wanted to take her baby doll out to lunch at a nearby restaurant with me (Dottie). Naturally, I had to bring my own baby doll. At six years old, Kristie already exhibited maternal instincts, attending to her "baby" in quite the motherly way. We sat our dolls in two individual high chairs, provided by an amused restaurant staff, and fed them lunch. Although we attracted quite a bit of attention in the restaurant, Kristie never batted an eye when she decided her baby needed a diaper change. While continuing to chat with me, she changed her baby's diaper right there on the lunch table!

A special birthday time activity for Julie was playing school. She turned our bedroom into a schoolroom for the day, while she played the role of math teacher. If I did not behave, Julie stood me in the corner and instructed me to write on the blackboard, *"I will listen to my teacher."* Julie sure kept me in line!

Trapping a bear was Matthew's adventure of choice for one of his Birthday Bonding activities. His birthday fell in the fall, so we had to wait for wintertime to celebrate his special wish. Matt needed *snow* to track bear footprints. Together we tramped through snowy woods, hunting for a bear trap. Not finding one, Matt was undeterred. He would make his own. Digging a large hole in the snow—large enough for a bear anyway—he laid broken tree branches over it, and waited for the bear that never came. Alas, rising early the next morning to examine the trap, we found it empty. Undaunted, that little boy never lost hope that one day he would trap a bear. Eventually, I was able to convince Matt that his bear was probably hibernating for the winter.

Traditions create a family identity that is as unique and special as each individual family.

For Amy's special birthday times with us, she wanted to have tea parties with her American Girl doll, Samantha. I brought my own special doll to our tea parties, a doll I named Lady Jane. Lady Jane taught us all good manners, such as placing our napkins in our laps, eating small bites, and not talking while we chewed. We pretended to have elegant ladies' conversations while serving each other tea and cookies. Sometimes Prince Charming (Pop-Pop) would join our tea parties when he was home for lunch.

With his inquisitive nature, Birthday Bonding for Ben revolved around education. Ben was a thinker. He often woke up in the morning with something *big* on his mind. One birthday morning Ben woke up with the *universe* on his mind! While Ben could be light-hearted and witty, on that particular morning, all he wanted to do was talk to us about planets. Roger can converse adeptly on any topic, so he and Ben spent that birthday engaged in man-talk!

Being a man of action, Andy's loves were go-carts, miniature golf, basketball, football, baseball, and anything else that involved a ball. Roger and I learned we would be wise to stretch and warm up before Andy's Birthday Bonding dates. Whatever the activity, he was hard to beat. I'm convinced that he *let* us win occasionally.

Even customs as simple and predictable as a birthday phone call and a small gift are meaningful to a grandchild.

For his special day with us, Stephen often chose to play anything that had to do with Spiderman. Sometimes he just wanted to climb trees together, walk the creek, or beat his grandfather at chess.

Melanie's Birthday Bonding activities also centered around sports. She loved to play soccer, but soon discovered we were not much competition for her. Not one to give up, Melanie suggested basketball instead. Agreeably, we formed imaginary basketball teams and played against one another. Melanie's teams were always tough for Mom-Mom to beat!

Our Birthday Bonding days have evolved into a favorite tradition among the grandchildren, filled with everything from hilarious laughter to heartfelt sharing. Whatever activities the children have proposed, we have learned to take them seriously. Chances are, they have been thinking about it all year!

In your family, you may want to let the children choose their own special birthday activities, as we have done, or, if they are short on ideas, you may want to facilitate things by writing a variety of Birthday Bonding activities on slips of paper and storing them in a decorated coffee can. Whenever a birthday rolls around, a grandchild can pull a surprise activity from the can for their special day.

Of course, Birthday Bonding activities are more limited when grandchildren live far away, as some of our grandchildren do. We find that we can still engage in special routines on their birthdays—we just need to be more creative and intentional about it. Even customs as simple and predictable as a birthday phone call and a small gift are meaningful to a grandchild and give them something special to anticipate from Grandma and Grandpa.

NEW TWISTS ON OLD TRADITIONS

Like most families, Christmas traditions are among our most treasured memories. Our family's favorite Christmas tradition has been our annual Christmas pageant.

The Christmas pageant tradition began in my family (Dottie's). My grandparents, aunts, and uncles joined us for the evening. We kids loved it. I have memories of my older brother as the pageant director, song leader, and piano player, whose role it was to play the piano between each scene while our family sang Christmas carols.

> **Like most families, Christmas traditions are among our most treasured memories.**

My mother made simple costumes from old pillowcases and remnants of fabric, my father read the Christmas story from the Bible, and my two brothers and I were the starring cast. For all its simplicity, our pageant was a wonderful memory.

As the next generation, Roger and I attempted our own Christmas pageant only once. With three girls, it was doomed from the start. No one wanted to be Joseph. So we let the tradition die with our generation.

As we became grandparents, however, our quiver rapidly filled with budding actors and actresses—enough to cast a Christmas pageant again! So the tradition was resurrected.

We created a makeshift stage in a wide doorway with a bed sheet serving as the perfect curtain. As my mother had done before me, I made simple, homemade costumes. We even had a stuffed donkey (inherited from a white elephant party several Christmases earlier). The donkey was perfect for "Mary" to ride into Bethlehem. Roger read a children's version of the Christmas story, while the grandchildren acted out each scene.

One memorable Christmas pageant was the year our youngest grandchild, Lianna, was two years old. As the littlest angel, she was dressed in a robe created from a pillowcase, with a halo made of gold tinsel and white cardboard wings. As the rest of the grandchildren played their roles with appropriate solemnity and dignity, a small little angel could be seen randomly toddling in and out of every scene unannounced. It was hard to hold back peals of laughter as we kept the video camera running.

We need to remember that Christmas for some families is not a joyful season of happy family memories.

Our Christmas pageant tradition has now been passed down to the fourth generation. As our grandchildren multiplied, the older ones transitioned into the audience, leaving room for the younger ones to enjoy the experience of acting. Some prolific years, we have had two Mary's and three angels propped in baby seats; some years the Christmas story has been read super-speed to accommodate fidgety children. But always, the Christmas pageant has left a lasting memory on young hearts.

CHRISTMAS DILEMMA

We need to remember that Christmas for some families is not a joyful season of happy family memories. Broken families, divided custody, and remarriages take their toll on holiday traditions. Christmas season can be a reminder of what has been lost. The result can be a sadness that permeates the holiday, gloom that is only intensified by the joy of others. There may now be additional sets of grandparents or remarried spouses to consider, multiplying the potential for stress and conflict. When strife compounds, it is the children who are hurt most of all. For some families, the issues may seem insurmountable. But, with the Lord *nothing* is impossible.

After several years of turmoil and strife, one family we know worked out a creative solution. This family took the children to visit each set of grandparents and former spouses separately during the month of December. By going to visit each one individually, jealousies were kept at bay, and everyone was able to spend quality time with the children. It was a sacrificial commitment on the part of the parents, but the children loved the arrangement. For them, it seemed that it was Christmas the whole month of December! Christmas Day itself became a

No family is without its trials and faults, but it is encouraging to know that holiday traditions can be powerful, healing opportunities to live the gospel before the searching, impressionable eyes of children.

special blessing for this blended family. They were able to spend the day together with their children. Their sacrifices earlier in the month became a blessing. The children grew up knowing their grandparents and building relationships with them, and the grandparents, likewise, were satisfied having spent quality time with their grandchildren.

No family is without its trials and faults, but it's encouraging to know that holiday traditions can be powerful, healing opportunities to *live* the gospel before the searching, impressionable eyes of children. Christmas can be a season to recall the day that the God of the universe reached down to rescue helpless sinners in need of a Savior. We can live the gospel by committing to be ambassadors of peace and reconciliation in and toward broken families in the next holiday season. What a legacy that would be!

A MEMORABLE EASTER TRADITION

On the eve of our Lord's crucifixion, knowing that His hour had come to leave this world, the final act He performed for His disciples was that of washing their feet, saying:

> *"Now that I, your Lord and Teacher, have washed your feet, you also should wash one another's feet. I have set you an example that you should do as I have done for you. . . . Now that you know these things, you will be blessed if you do them"* (John 13:14–17 NIV).

The gospel story does not end with the crucifixion; it ends with a glorious resurrection to a new life!

One family we know has an Easter tradition of following Jesus' example of washing one another's feet as music plays, and the Easter story is read. It is a time for those present—children included—to humble themselves and seek forgiveness from one another for wrongs committed; it is a time to reconcile with one another and start anew. The gospel story does not end with the crucifixion; it ends with a glorious resurrection to a new life!

We will never forget the first time we shared an Easter tradition with friends of the Jewish faith who are true believers in their Messiah, *Yeshua.* They celebrate the Passover Seder on Easter, pointing to Jesus as the fulfillment of the Old Testament prophecies. It is a special blessing for us to share Easter with Jewish believers in the Messiah, unified as one new body in Jesus Christ!

The most exciting part of the Passover Seder was when the grandfather, the patriarch of the family, picked up the third cup of wine, the Cup of Redemption. He explained that for thousands of years, this particular cup of wine was never to be touched. The Jewish people believed that when the Messiah came, only He would drink from this cup.

> **Think back on some of the memories you had as a child . . . then refashion those memories with your grandchildren.**

And that was exactly what Jesus did. We can only imagine the shock on the disciples' faces when Jesus picked up the Cup of Redemption, blessed it, and gave it to them saying, *"Drink from it, all of you. This is my blood of the covenant, which is poured out for many for the forgiveness of sins"* (Matthew 26:27–28 NIV). Truly Jesus was announcing to His disciples that He was their long-awaited Messiah, whose atoning death would bring salvation to all who believe.

CREATIVE FAMILY TRADITIONS

Think back on some of the memories you had as a child or some of the special moments you shared with your own children. Then refashion those memories with your grandchildren. There is special fun in saying to a grandchild, "This was something your mommy (or daddy) used to love doing!"

If you are looking for ideas to create new family traditions for your grandchildren, try plugging the words "family traditions" into an Internet search. Literally hundreds of ideas will pop up. We have included a few sample ideas in this chapter; however, we think you will find that you already have some pretty great ideas of your own!

If some of these traditions seem simplistic to you, remember that their purpose is to provide a backdrop for rich, meaningful relationships—and that is a pearl of great worth!

- **Fourth of July Battle of the Snowballs:** This annual tradition is not only a family favorite, but a neighborhood favorite as well. It will take a bit of forethought, but it will be well worth it when you see the delight it creates! You will want to prepare by making snowballs with your grandchildren after a freshly fallen snow. Make as many snowballs as your freezer will hold—whether only a bowl full or an entire freezer full—it is up to you. (Note: It's important that the snow be fresh and free of twigs or debris, as these may clog your freezer.)

If some of these traditions seem simplistic to you, remember that their purpose is to provide a backdrop for rich, meaningful relationships—and that is a pearl of great worth!

On the Fourth of July, when the temperature is soaring, pull out your snowballs and prepare to cool off with a good old-fashioned snowball fight with your grandkids! You will want to stage your snowball fight in a location where you are sure to attract a lot of attention, as neighboring children (and likely grown-ups, too) will want to join the fun! The street is a great location, if your street is not too busy. The sound of frozen snowballs exploding on hot July pavement is quite exhilarating. And don't be surprised if you hear comments like, "I wish *my* grandparents did this with me!" This hilarious tradition is likely to grow each year as more and more neighbors decide to join the fun. Encourage them to bring their own snowballs next year! (One word of caution: freezer snowballs can be quite hard; you will want to caution your eager contestants, "No fastballs; no snowballs above the neck; and no hitting cars!")

- **A Tradition of Serving:** Why not begin a Christmas, Thanksgiving, or Easter morning tradition of serving at a homeless shelter? Find a local ministry that serves breakfast or lunch to homeless people on holidays and volunteer together with your grandchildren to help make and serve the meal. This tradition is guaranteed to leave a lasting impression on your grandchildren, and perhaps on you as well. It is always enlightening for children to discover that there are other children who are homeless.

- **Easter Egg Tradition:** This tradition requires you to rise very early on Easter morning to pull off your mischief under the cloak of darkness—but that is half the fun! In preparation before Easter, you will want to boil and color eggs together with your grandchildren. What makes this tradition meaningful is decorating the eggs with the true meaning of Easter. One family we know writes on each egg before laying them on neighbors' doorsteps: "Jesus loves you so much . . . that He stretched out His arms and died." Come up with your own special words or Bible verses—but be sure to make a *lot* of eggs! Before your neighbors arise on Easter morning, you and your grandchildren can sneak quietly down your street laying one egg on each neighbor's doorstep.

- **Christmas Eve Tradition:** Consider an annual tradition of giving each grandchild a new set of pajamas on Christmas Eve, to wear as they sleep under the Christmas tree with their parents. It is extra special if you leave the Christmas lights on all night and let the children fall asleep to soft Christmas music.

- **Painting the Barn Tradition:** The next time the kids act bored, announce, "Time to paint the barn!" An all-time favorite of which children never seem to tire is an outdoor house-painting event—using wide paintbrushes and buckets of water as "paint." With the buckets of water, paint the house, paint the deck, paint the garage door, paint Grandpa napping on the porch, paint anything that holds still! Grandpa and Grandma may want to join in on this one, or let the kids "paint" while you relax! If the kids are really into it, pay a visit to your local paint supply store and stock up on authentic painter's gear to keep stashed and ready in the garage: painter's caps, aprons, empty paint cans, small rollers, and brushes. The best part about this activity is that when most surfaces become wet, they change color. Young children are convinced they are really painting, while older and wiser children still enjoy feeling like Michelangelo for a day. When the surfaces dry, start all over again! Your grandchildren will have a blast—and you will have the cleanest house on the block.

- **Pizza Kitchen Tradition:** When the grandchildren come to visit, make it a treat to let them create their own pizzas. Teenagers especially love this tradition. When it comes to food, they seem to appear out of the woodwork! In preparation, cover a table with a wipeable or disposable tablecloth for easy clean up. Make your own pizza dough, or buy ready-made, and form individual-size pizzas for each grandchild. Let each one decorate his or her pizza with toppings. Even the youngest love to finger paint in the sauce! You don't need a lot of topping choices for younger children, but teenagers may relish the freedom to be wild and creative at Grandma's house! If they want to put chocolate chips and whipped cream on their pizza, why not? (Our only house rule: *"If you make it—you eat it!"* Fair enough!)

- **Board Game Tradition:** Board games played by traditional rules are always fun and have a distinct way of fostering a spirit of camaraderie—but try surprising the kids with some interesting variations every now and then. For example, you can play a round where you make up your own silly rules. For older children and teens, each player can add in one new rule that everyone has to follow. We have friends who especially like doing this with *Uno.* They have dubbed their family version, *"Extreme Uno!"* Challenge your grandchildren to make up a new card game, and teach you how to play it. For your part, you can search YouTube for some stunning card tricks and really impress your grandchildren!

> **Your grandchildren will have a blast—and you will have the cleanest house on the block.**

- **Movie Star Tradition:** With nothing more than a cell-phone video camera and a computer, this generation has the marvelous ability to create their own original movies. Many kids are surprisingly adept at using computer-generated special effects and dubbing in background music. All they need are a great idea, a fun script—and willing actors. And that is where grandparents come into play! Making a video together with your grandchildren is a truly memorable way to spend an afternoon. The only thing more fun is posting it online and watching it again and again and again! You will have left an enduring, tangible legacy.

- **Snack Island Tradition:** Few things have the power to bring a smile to the faces of children of any age like edible treats. Have a special spot in your kitchen—a cupboard, a drawer, a corner counter or shelf—for goodies, treats, and special delectables. Grandma's kitchen takes on an almost magical air when kids have a special place that is kept stocked just for them. To create an enticing "Snack Island," fill clear containers or small baskets of various sizes with colorful, miniature snack items. Healthy choices can certainly be part of the array: peanuts, dried fruit, granola bars, graham crackers, etc. Arrange the containers decoratively. An Internet search (Google or Google Images) will yield some wonderfully creative ideas to make a more elaborate Snack Island if you are so inspired. After all, goodies and treats are what grandparents are known for! We call it "Snack Island," but it may be the closest thing to *Paradise Island* in the eyes of a child!

> **Whatever your family traditions, do not be afraid to announce a Cold Turkey Fast from electronic devices at your home during special activities.**

Whatever your family traditions, do not be afraid to announce a *Cold Turkey Fast* from electronic devices at your home during special activities. This is *not* a punishment—it is a *blessing!* It is because you value your grandchildren as little people, and you desire to spend quality time with them. We certainly cannot argue that the Internet, cell phones, and handheld electronic devices possess a magnetic allure, but that attraction can be counterproductive to human interaction. Believe it or not, young people have popularized a new way of relating to others, which is becoming increasingly acceptable. It's called *phubbing.* Phubbing is defined as snubbing whomever one is with at the moment, pretending to listen, while staring at a cell phone.

Your pause from cell phones, social media, and other distractions that preempt human interaction may be for any period of time that you choose—but don't be afraid to set limits. For older teens, you may want to allow free phone time after 9:00 p.m., as an example. This tradition means you will have to put your own phone away, too, while you are interacting with the grandchildren, except for phone calls to Mom and Dad. Ironically, after the initial shock and resistance subside, many teens actually appreciate being challenged to function without their constant electronic companions. They discover that they actually enjoy interactive, human activities!

THOUGHTS TO PONDER

Let your grandchildren see you serving others. It speaks volumes to children to let them see you living the gospel by reaching out to others, serving others, and showing God's love and kindness in real and practical ways. The example you model with your life will speak louder to them than any sermon. Serving together with your grandchildren is one of the most rewarding and memorable traditions you can pass down. So don't clear your calendar when the grandchildren come to visit. Instead, let them see your servant's heart, and let them participate with you.

If there is a widow or widower on your street, a single mother, or a young mother with a new baby, invite one of your grandchildren over to make and deliver a simple meal to them. Bake cookies together and deliver them to someone whose spirit could use a lift. Of course, you will want to let your little helpers lick the bowl and nibble the cookies as you bake! Take one or two of your grandchildren with you to do some yard work or plant flowers for an elderly couple. In the end, your grandchildren will remember these experiences far longer than they will remember the presents they received that Christmas.

OUR PRAYER

Dear heavenly Father,

Little did we know that the blessed return on our investment into the lives of our children would be grandchildren. They belong to You, Lord, so we entrust them into Your capable, Fatherly hands. May You bless their days and protect them from evil in these trying times.

It is our prayer, Lord, that You will equip us to rise up as leaders in our families, and not be deterred by the influence of the enemy, who seeks to sabotage Your good and perfect ways. Would You enable us, by Your Spirit, to create lasting family traditions that will continue through the generations. May You knit our families together with bonds of laughter and tears, joy, and shared memories.

Father, we know that it grieves Your heart to see fractures in families. But You are a reconciler. Times without number You have responded to the earnest prayers of grandparents and have restored fractured relationships in families. Will You write a new song—a song of reconciliation and hope—to families that are hurting? Will You revive and restore families to Your original design? And will You look after the children and invite them come to You? For of such is the kingdom of heaven.

We ask these things in Jesus' name.

Amen.

11 · DISCIPLINING GRANDCHILDREN: STAY IN YOUR LANE

*All your children shall be taught by the L*ORD*,*
And great shall be the peace of your children.

—Isaiah 54:13

You know the scene. We, too, are all too familiar with it. Your sweet-faced-grandchild-with-the-big-innocent-eyes has just committed a behavior that is unacceptable. There is no denying it, nor overlooking it. That is when the thoughts start to collide in your brain. An appropriate response is clearly needed. Yet there you stand, paralyzed by the war that has begun to wage in your mind. We've been there!

On the one hand, your *rational* brain prompts you, "You have raised this child's parent. Surely that qualifies you to interject your unsolicited advice, right?"

On the other hand, your *relational* brain counters, "But you are not the parent here. It is not your place to correct this child."

Perhaps you don't want to overstep your boundaries. Most likely you are not anxious to create conflict in the family. Brain collisions occur as you wrestle with your options in the heat of the moment.

Meanwhile, an impish little face is staring at you, waiting to see what you will do. What is a grandparent to do?

I wish we could say that grandparenting has been all mountaintop experiences and warm, fuzzy memories for us, but alas, that is not the reality of life. Children are children the world around. They know just where to push a grown-up's buttons. Grandchildren can be the most effective little button-pushers God ever created, albeit with a touch of situational irony. At the end of the day, grandchildren can be sent home to their parents!

To be honest, our most challenging area in grandparenting has been found in the big D territory—*Discipline.* One does not have to spend very many afternoons with a pint-sized being to know that healthy discipline and boundaries are an essential part of the equation. Yet so many conflicting desires battle within us.

> **Our most challenging area in grandparenting has been found in the big D territory—Discipline.**

In our early years of grandparenting, we were not quite sure what our discipline boundaries ought to look like or how to establish them. *Which behaviors should we correct? What should we overlook?* We certainly did not want to cause conflict in our family. To be quite candid, we wanted our grandchildren to *like* us. We even had an insecure fear that if we said "no" to our grandchildren, they might not want to spend time with us. Heaven forbid *that* should happen! In addition, it was downright difficult at times to say "no" to an adorable little face!

You would think that years of parenting our own daughters would have better prepared us to be grandparents, but they had not. Putting on our grandparenting caps was a whole new ballgame for us. It had its own learning curve—and prior experience had little to do with it. In short, *we* were not the parents in this inning of the game.

Through the years, Roger and I have learned not to discipline the children directly. Yes, we set boundaries in our home, but when it came to disciplining the children, we tactfully offered our observations about the children's behavior to their parents, behind the scenes. We let their parents handle things from there. And then we prayed for our grandchildren.

*All your children shall be taught by the L*ORD*, And great shall be the peace of your children* (Isaiah 54:13).

The beautiful promise of Isaiah 54 has come to rest over us like a dove, bringing peace to our hearts and our home. We leave plenty of room for the Lord to do His work. What a privilege we have as grandparents to be observant, loving eyes into the lives of the generations that follow in our footsteps. Our observations as we relate to our grandchildren become golden opportunities for us to take to the Lord in prayer. And *that* is a powerful legacy for any grandparent!

Letting the parents *be* the parents builds bonds of trust and respect all the way around. It defers to their leadership. It honors them as the heads of their own households. And it has taught us to put holy, restraining zippers on our lips! Many times, instead of speaking out of our human impulses, we have turned the matter into the substance of our prayers.

> **Letting the parents be the parents builds bonds of trust and respect all the way around.**

Even now, the potential for conflict still crouches tenaciously at our door. We have learned through the years and through our mistakes that the crucial lesson is to *stay in our lane.* Each member of our family has his or her own role to fill. Our role is that of *grandparents*. We have passed the baton to our children to be the *parents*. How much strife and conflict we avoid by being content to stay in our own lane and accept our role in this season of life. This elementary principle has profoundly affected our family relationships.

KEEPING THE LINES OF COMMUNICATION OPEN

Since the time they were young, we have instilled in our grandchildren the message that the door to our ears is always open to them. They know they have the freedom to talk to Roger and me about anything. We will listen and respect them as little people—treasures who are valued greatly by God and by us—but there *is* a catch. Our grandchildren also know that we will be truthful in talking to their parents. Very simply, we keep the lines of communication open and honest, all the way around. We have been candid with all our grandchildren about this right from the start.

We have instilled in our grandchildren the message that the door to our ears is always open to them.

With younger grandchildren, when we felt their parents should be involved in a situation, we made it our practice to say to the children, "We feel this is something we need to share with your parents. After all, they are your parents." We did not tattletale behind their backs; we let them know up front that we would be talking to their parents.

As the children grew older, when there were behavior issues, we encouraged them to talk to their parents themselves. I might say something simple like, "Honey, you really should talk to your parents about this when you go home." Years later, we learned from some of our grandchildren that this gave them a comforting sense of security, knowing that there was a consistent standard, and that they could not behave one way at home and another way at Mom-Mom and Pop-Pop's house. This was one way of demonstrating our love for them—and they felt that love.

In addition to strengthening the bonds of trust, maintaining open communication between our children, our grandchildren, and us has given Roger and me a platform from which to speak into the grandchildren's lives. This bridge into their lives has proven invaluable, as our grandchildren have entered into the tumultuous teenage and independent young adult years. If a grandchild confided in us issues that potentially needed parental guidance or correction, Roger and I listened carefully and offered our input. However, by the end of the conversations, we still encouraged them to talk to their parents about the issue. After that, we stepped back to the sidelines, leaving the ball and the final decision in their court.

A word of caution may be in order here. As we build trusting relationships and open communication with our grandchildren, there is a temptation to desire to be the "trusted confidante." It is important that we *not* encourage the children to talk to us confidentially. For example, a grandchild may come to us saying something like, "I feel like you're the only one I can talk to," or "Please don't tell my parents this . . ." For the sake of love and integrity, we do not want to become a divisive factor between parents and children. We want to be a positive, strengthening influence in family relationships. Once again, it is important to know our lane—and stay in it!

For the sake of love and integrity, we do not want to become a divisive factor between parents and children.

SOME PRACTICAL ADVICE

Perhaps, like us, you dutifully childproofed your home when you were raising your children, all the while entertaining in your imagination visions of the beautiful home you would have *when the children were grown.* Enter grandchildren upon the scene—those precious little bundles of inquisitive, non-stop energy! From the time they first learned to walk upright, we found we needed a few extra doses of vitamins and a good pair of sneakers to keep up with them! Following a toddler around for a day was exhausting—but we have to admit, it was a *good* tired feeling. We sure loved those little ones!

As grandparents, we decided to avoid unnecessary confrontations and needless accidents by stashing valuables and breakables out of sight. Much to our joy, we discovered that the relationships we built with our grandchildren were far more valuable treasures than our home décor. Stowing away fragile items while our grandchildren were young had the added benefit of freeing our daughters and sons-in-law from anxiety over the inevitable accidents.

Our second step was to once again childproof our home with safety gadgets, ready for the next batch of little people in our lives. Back on went the electric outlet covers, doorknob locks, and cabinet latches. We were especially vigilant to ensure that battery compartments on toys were securely screwed shut and checked regularly. Small children, naïve to the danger, could pop those batteries into their mouths in the blink of an eye. We moved cleaning supplies out of the reach of inquisitive little hands, particularly those cute dishwashing detergent packs that resemble pillows and are, for some odd reason, particularly inviting—and poisonous.

We decided to avoid unnecessary confrontations and needless accidents by stashing valuables and breakables out of sight.

By the time the children turned preschool age, their need for correction in our home became unavoidable. As much as we dreaded correcting them, we knew we had no choice. It was what *love* dictated. We learned to conceal our chuckles over their cute antics at times and do the meaningful work of correcting them when necessary.

We are so thankful to others who shared their wisdom with us and encouraged us along the way. One of the most helpful pieces of advice we were given was, "Say what you mean, and mean what you say—or don't say it at all." That wise maxim guided us smoothly through many potentially rough waters. We wished we had known it when we were parenting!

We also created a list of house rules for Mom-Mom and Pop-Pop's house. Your list will probably look different from ours, but we intentionally kept our list short and simple:

- no dirty shoes on furniture

- no complaining or arguing with a sibling (Offenders will be separated from playing together.)

- put away toys after playing with them

We shared our list of house rules with the children's parents, so they could refresh their children's memories before bringing them to visit.

Our system of childproofing our home, establishing a few behavior boundaries, and including our grown children in the plan worked effectively for us. As our family grew with more and more new grandchildren (and great-grandchildren!), Roger and I also continued to grow and discover more about this wonderful calling of grandparenting!

> **"Say what you mean, and mean what you say—or don't say it at all."**

REINFORCING PARENTS' RULES

In our family, we found it particularly useful to know the routines and behavior expectations in our grown children's homes. We made it our standard practice to respect their wishes and enforce their standards when their children were in our home. Sometimes we just *had* to push the limit with bedtime stories, though. One bedtime story was never enough!

Our grandchildren quickly got the hint that we knew what their parents' expectations were. By sticking to their familiar routines and standards, it not only gave the children a sense of constancy and stability, but it also gave us some leverage. We had only to remind them, "Do you remember what Mommy and Daddy say about that?" On many occasions, that rhetorical question was a lifesaver!

We learned to choose our "battles" with the children judiciously and to decide which hills we were willing to die on when it came to managing behavior. Even so, we occasionally needed to make use of a time-out chair. That little chair was heaven-sent. It was amazing how the rest of the siblings transformed instantly into angelic creatures when they saw an unfortunate offender banished to the time-out chair!

> **We learned to choose our "battles" with the children judiciously and to decide which hills we were willing to die on when it came to managing behavior.**

In summary, our guiding principles for disciplining grandchildren were simple: show respect for our sons-in-law and daughters, leave discipline to the parents, keep the lines of communication open—and stay in our own lane.

TEA-TIME TALKS

We recognize that every family and every situation is uniquely different, as varied and distinctive as families are. There is no one-size-fits-all formula when it comes to grandparenting. We have included in this chapter a few of the many personal stories that have been shared with us over innumerable cups of tea throughout the years. Although details differ and names have been changed, the basic storylines ring surprisingly similar: grandparents longing to be good grandparents.

JOAN'S STORY: TEARS OF A GRANDMOTHER

There was a little girl,
And she had a little curl
Right in the middle of her forehead.
When she was good,
She was very, very good,
And when she was bad, she was _____.

Most of us can finish this familiar little ditty by Henry Wadsworth Longfellow from memory. But for my longtime friend Joan, this was more than a lighthearted rhyme. The joy she had anticipated as a grandmother had transformed into something "horrid." Sitting across my kitchen table staring into a cup of tea, Joan's trembling voice betrayed the depth of her emotion.

Joan had waited ten long years to become a grandmother. By the time her first and only grandchild came along, Joan had high hopes for a rewarding relationship. She quickly became deeply attached to little Vicki. Not wanting to miss out on a single joy of this new grandparenting experience, Joan indulged her granddaughter in many a whim and demand. After all, isn't that what grandparents are for?

The joy she had anticipated as a grandmother had transformed into something "horrid."

Vicki soon earned the nickname of Little Princess. And believe me, she played the role of a princess expertly. Vicki led Grandma Joan around like a princess with her courtiers. Whatever Princess wanted, Princess was given. Joan never said "no" and never disciplined Vicki. At first, Joan thought it was innocently cute, but things deteriorated when Princess Vicki began to talk back to her loyal subject—her grandmother. And Joan permitted it. After all, isn't that what a doting grandmother is for?

151

Pausing for a sip of tea, Joan collected her thoughts. Soon the rest of her story tumbled from her heart.

Joan had asked three-year-old Vicki to pick up her shoes and put them in her room. With her hands on her hips and in a tone of disgust that belied her young age, Vicki shouted, "I don't want anyone telling me what to do!"

Joan was stunned. When had her little princess transformed into a toad? Joan was speechless. It is one thing to deal with belligerent behavior in one's own child, but quite another thing with a grandchild. Feeling confused and brokenhearted, Joan silently retreated to her rocking chair for a time of quiet contemplation and composure. Vicki followed her. As Joan gently rocked back and forth, Vicki chattered on and on as if nothing out of the ordinary had just occurred.

Love compels us to put our hearts out there again and again when it is for the good of another.

My heart went out to my friend as I sympathized with her struggle. Somehow, the people we love the most are the ones who have the greatest capacity to cause us pain, as little Vicki was causing her grandmother. And yet, love compels us to put our hearts out there again and again when it is for the good of another.

Joan and I both sat silently sipping our tea as I wrestled with the heaviness of the burden my friend's heart was carrying.

Wisdom and discernment were definitely needed here, along with gloves of gentleness. It was difficult to know where to begin to help Joan because the fears that tainted her actions were deeply ingrained in her heart; yet her motives were pure. Quite simply, Joan was afraid to discipline her granddaughter. Nevertheless, it's never too late to hit the *reset* button and start afresh. It was not too late for Joan to begin a new family legacy, beginning with herself. After all, the Lord offers us fresh opportunities and new mercies every morning.

Joan was quick to admit that the unhealthy patterns with her granddaughter had begun with herself. She had unwittingly permitted Vicki to assume the place of authority in their relationship. Their roles had been reversed, with three-year-old Vicki acting like the one in charge. Joan agreed that it was time to take back the reins of leadership in a healthy way.

I listened attentively as Joan finished her story. Then I offered, "I know how you feel, dear. I had a similar experience with one of my own grandchildren. The next time Vicki talks back to you, why don't you try responding to her matter-of-factly and firmly, 'Grandma loves you very much, Vicki, and that is why I will not permit you to speak to me that way.' You can add, 'Remember how Mommy told you that you were to obey Grandma? Now, you scoot over there and pick up your shoes and put them back in your room. Then you and I can have story time.'"

The next time I saw Joan, she greeted me ecstatically, "You know, Dottie, I can hardly believe it! It worked! Ever since that day, Vicki has been much more compliant and obedient. She actually does what I ask her to do. Until recently, I had never spoken to her in that firm but gentle tone of voice. I said what I meant, and I meant what I said. It's almost like Vicki feels reassured knowing who is in charge when her mother is away."

The Lord offers us fresh opportunities and new mercies every morning.

Joan's role as a grandmother is still a journey in process. Day by day, her greatest place of peace and comfort is on her knees before the Lord. And her greatest place of joy is in her rocking chair with her granddaughter on her lap, telling Vicki stories that she prays will reach her heart.

MAGGIE'S STORY: HARSH JUDGMENTS

Although Maggie and I had known each other for years, on this particular morning that Maggie stopped over for a chat, her eyes refused to connect with mine. I knew something was wrong. At last, her eyes met mine with a look that pleaded for help.

"I don't know what to do," Maggie lamented. "My daughter is overly permissive in her parenting, and my grandchildren are out of control. You have no idea how rowdy and undisciplined they can be, Dottie. When they leave, it's like a cyclone has hit. I really don't know what to do anymore. Do you have any ideas?"

I knew Maggie was devoted to her daughter and adored her grandchildren. Yet grandparenting was not at all what she had expected. And it certainly was not delivering the joy for which she had hoped.

Grandparenting was not at all what she had expected. And it certainly was not delivering the joy for which she had hoped.

Maggie's daughter, Janni, no doubt had her hands full, with four children all under the age of six. Her daughter did not believe in spanking and feared being reported to the authorities if she did. As a result, she was a yeller. Janni frequently threatened her children with consequences, but she rarely followed through. Her own mother had not raised Janni that way, but the culture spoke louder to Janni than her mother's wisdom. Consequently, it was nightmarish when the four grandchildren came to visit.

Maggie and I shared many cups of tea, discussing how she might help her daughter to understand the difficulty of having her children in her home. It was clearly a sensitive situation with no easy answers.

"Janni is an adult now—and a mother who is responsible for raising four children. Have you tried talking to her openly about the situation as you see it?" I ventured.

"I have tried that many times, Dottie. We don't get anywhere. Janni doesn't want to listen. She blames me for being too fussy and demanding. Do you think that wanting a degree of order and respect in my home is being too strict, Dottie?"

"No, I don't think so at all. But you have to remember that we are from another generation, Maggie. Training children to show respect is still the goal—but we may have to be more patient and tolerant in the way we go about it. After all, we are not the parents here. If you lose your relationship with your daughter and grandchildren over this, you will have lost a golden opportunity to be influential in their lives."

Maggie quietly mulled this over for a while before responding.

"Perhaps I *am* being too fussy. Janni told me that it might be better if I come to *her* house to see the children. It might work better that way, but it breaks my heart not to be able to have the children to myself sometimes. I want so much to be a good grandmother to them."

"You *are* a good grandmother, dear," I encouraged Maggie. "You love those kids. You pray for them, and you desire what is good for them. Persevere patiently, my friend. Try not to grow weary in showing acts of kindness to your family. The day will come when the children will want to spend special time with you at your home. When that day comes, perhaps you can invite them over one at a time. If you can't reach them *en masse*, perhaps you can reach them individually, one by one.

> **"Persevere patiently, my friend. Do not grow weary in showing acts of kindness to your family."**

"For the time being, your grandchildren are still so young. It might be better for everyone if you took your daughter's suggestion and visited them in *their* home. That way, you can leave whenever you want to. Do you see where I'm going with this?"

"Yes, Dottie. I think I'm starting to see what you mean. You're saying, 'Don't push the envelope at this point in time. Don't try so hard to win the battle, but lose the whole war.' I can win the battle over disciplining my grandchildren in my home—but lose my opportunity to build relationships with them, right?"

"You've got it, Maggie. Let this battle go. Don't forget—your relationship with your daughter means a lot, too, in this early season of parenting."

"I think you're right, Dottie. I'm so glad we had this talk. It isn't easy being a grandmother, is it?"

"Hey, girlfriend, when you figure this whole grandparenting thing out, let *me* know!"

> **"You're saying . . . I can win the battle over disciplining my grandchildren in my home—but lose my opportunity to build relationships with them, right?"**

As we wrapped up our teatime, Maggie confessed, "I have to admit I've been focusing on *fixing* this discipline problem. I imagine my daughter has been feeling my critical judgments for not raising her children the way I think she ought to. I think I owe her an apology."

"I know your heart's motive has not been to be critical, Maggie. But Janni doesn't. Why don't you go over and have a cup of tea with her while the children are napping? You can clear the air in person. I suspect Janni will be relieved—and appreciative of your humility."

HELEN'S STORY: A HOUSE DIVIDED

Helen's grandparenting dilemma was quite different. As she sat with me over a cup of tea, her gaze danced furtively around the room before settling on her clenched hands in her lap. I had not remembered seeing Helen so nervous before. I wondered what was troubling her. Anxiously, Helen began to unload her story.

Helen was grieved by the strict manner in which her daughter-in-law, Kathy, disciplined her two grandchildren, Danny and Tim. In Helen's opinion, Kathy was far too strict with the boys. She barely gave them room to breathe. It seemed to my friend Helen that Kathy was smothering the boys with constant corrections and reprimands.

Danny and Tim were dear little five-year-old twins. And they were all boy, through and through. They loved to play-wrestle together, until Kathy commanded, "Boys, stop your fighting right now!"

If the boys responded defensively, "But Mommy, we aren't fi—" Kathy would squash their defense before they could finish.

"Stop it *right now,* or you will be punished."

It seemed to Helen that the twins were always being punished for one boyish behavior or another. "Kathy obviously doesn't understand how boys play," Helen thought. "She was raised in a family of four girls. They probably played quietly with dolls and coloring books," Helen imagined.

The boys' relentless energy kept Kathy on edge. Whenever they did not do what she expected, she threatened to punish them. The mere sound of the word *punish* frightened the boys enough to obey.

As the grandmother, Helen thought it was her duty to intervene on the boys' behalf. She decided to speak to her son, Ken, believing he would understand and be sympathetic to her perspective on the matter. After all, Ken was the more laid back and relaxed parent. As they say, "Opposites attract."

Helen was taken aback by her son's response when she expressed her concerns over Kathy's childrearing approach.

"Mom, thank you for your concern, but the boys are doing just fine. Kathy is only trying to keep the boys' behavior in check."

Well, that was a surprise. Helen had not anticipated that Ken would support his wife when Kathy was clearly in the wrong. She decided the situation warranted her pressing in a little harder.

"I realize that, Ken, but don't you think Kathy is a little too stern with the boys? Can't you speak to her about showing them more grace? She is on them for everything. When they wrestle, she thinks they're fighting. If their clothes get dirty playing outside, she sends them inside to change. Don't you think that's going a bit too far?"

"Mom, please drop it. Kathy is a good mom. She is doing her best. I would appreciate it if you would encourage her instead of criticizing her."

Helen couldn't just "drop it." Her grievances on behalf of the boys had been building inside like a pressure cooker. Her next words steamed out of her mouth uncontrollably. "No wonder those boys are so fearful around adults. They're even afraid of *me*, Ken."

"I don't want to talk about this anymore, Mom." Ken turned his back to his mother and walked into the house.

It was to be a day of fresh beginnings in many ways. The Lord had already begun to direct her steps down a new path.

Numbly, Helen excused herself and headed for her car, vowing silently to herself that she would never bring up the subject of discipline again. Ken could not have known how difficult this confrontation had been for his mother. Helen's husband had died the year before the twins were born, leaving Helen feeling acutely alone. Her life revolved around those grandchildren.

I noticed Helen's hands clenched so tightly in her lap that I could see her knuckles turning white. Her lower lip quivered, and her eyes pooled with silent tears as she quietly finished telling me her story.

Upon arriving home, Helen rushed upstairs to her bedroom and flung herself across the bed, at last allowing her pent up tears to flow. "I miss you so very much, Jerry," she sobbed to the memory of her late husband. "If you were still here with me, *you* would know what to do.

You would take those boys fishing, play ball with them, and, yes, you would even wrestle with them."

That night as Helen lay in her bed, still troubled by the day's events, she poured out an appeal to the Lord. "Lord Jesus, I need Your wisdom. I don't want to interfere any more in the way Kathy and Ken choose to discipline their boys, nor do I want to be a divisive force between them in their marriage. They made a vow before You to 'leave their father and mother and cleave to one another.' I want to be a strong support to them in their marriage and in their family. Please help me to know my place." It wasn't long before a blanket of peaceful, healing sleep enveloped her.

Helen awoke refreshed the next morning, her heart filled with new joy, and her mind filled with new revelation and a deeper level of understanding. It was to be a day of fresh beginnings in many ways. The Lord had already begun to direct her steps down a new path.

She saw for the first time that their love for each other provided a strong sense of security for their sons.

First, Helen thanked the Lord for Ken's marriage to Kathy. She saw for the first time that their love for each other provided a strong sense of security for their sons.

Second, she reached out to Kathy in supportive and encouraging ways, looking for opportunities to compliment Kathy on her desire to be a good mother.

Third, Helen was convicted that she had been critical and judgmental of Kathy's parenting. It had never occurred to her that Kathy was simply trying to be a good parent, the best way she knew how. Helen determined to try to understand things from Kathy's perspective. As a way of beginning a new legacy, Helen knew she needed to talk openly and graciously with Kathy and Ken and ask them to forgive her for being so critical. She even invited them to bring their concerns to her in the future any time they felt she was again being overly critical.

Helen's honesty and humility opened a brand-new door in her relationship with her son and daughter-in-law. Helen regularly took the boys for outings to the park and back to her home for lunch, where she allowed them to play-wrestle and be boys. Out came the games, puzzles and story books, and of course, Grandma's special cookies. If one of the twins spilled a drink or accidentally made a mess, Helen was quick to respond, "That's all right. Grandma can clean it up. Would you like to help me?"

With the Lord's help, a house divided can be unified once again.

A GRANDFATHER'S INFLUENCE: A HEART OF GOLD

There are many ways a man can bond with his grandsons, but our next story is an unusual tale of a grandfather's influence on his granddaughter.

Thirteen-year-old Missy was visiting her grandparents for the weekend. Grandfather Gary and Grandma Emma often encouraged Missy to spend time with other children in the neighborhood when she visited them. That particular Saturday afternoon, Missy was invited to a neighborhood pool party. Gary, Emma, and Missy all agreed it would be a great opportunity for Missy to make some new friends. Excitedly, she raced upstairs to change into her swimsuit.

Bouncing excitedly back down the stairs, Missy was stopped dead in her tracks by the gruff voice of her grandfather.

"Whoooaa—no granddaughter of mine is going out of my house dressed like that!" And he meant it. Gary loved his granddaughter, and out of his protective love, he did not hesitate to speak up when he had convictions about her welfare.

It was an awkward moment for Missy—and completely unexpected. Not knowing what to do, she turned and darted back up the stairs to look for her grandmother.

"What's the matter, Missy?" asked Grandma Emma, seeing the look of bewilderment on her face.

"Why is Grandpa being so old-fashioned? He said I can't wear this bathing suit to the pool party."

"Sweetheart, Grandpa is not being old-fashioned. He loves you, and that's just his way of protecting you."

"Protecting me? From what?"

"We'll talk with your mother about it later. For now, your grandfather is right. That bathing suit will never do. Let's make a quick trip to the store and look for a new one together, shall we?"

> **With the Lord's help, a house divided can be unified once again.**

It did not take Grandma and Missy long to find a new swimsuit that was agreeable to them both—one with a lot more material. On the quiet drive home, Missy asked uncertainly, "Do you think my new swimsuit will meet with Grandpa's approval?"

"I think so," Grandma Emma assured her. "But I think he will be even *more* pleased that you showed him respect him and didn't argue to have your own way."

Grandpa Gary's tone wasn't always the most loving, but his heart toward his grandchildren was as good as gold. And his grandchildren respected him.

GRANDPARENTS: PILLARS OF STRENGTH IN HARD TIMES

One of the most tragic signs of the times is the crumbling of families and the devastating impact it has on its innocent victims—children. How is a grandparent to respond when this situation comes to pass in one's own family?

These are the heartbreaking times in life when grandparents are genuinely needed to step into the role of disciplinarian, to replace an absentee parent or to support an emotionally devastated parent.

Twenty-five years into their marriage, after having successfully raised their own family, Jacob and Sara found themselves distraught when divorce struck their daughter's home. They wrestled to find their place as grandparents, torn between grim options, of which none was ideal. Regardless of the many hurdles and hardships they knew they would face, Jacob and Sara knew they could not stand by helplessly and do nothing. Jessica needed their help to raise her two young children. Jacob and Sara chose the path of unconditional love and welcomed their daughter and grandchildren back into their home in their time of need. No one anticipated that the arrangement would stretch into six long years.

> **Regardless of the many hurdles and hardships they knew they would face, they knew they could not stand by helplessly and do nothing.**

At first, it was extremely challenging for Sara to step back into the role of mothering her grown daughter. To complicate things further, Sara was ill-equipped for the role of grandmother, with the children's own mother living in the same household. Put the two together under one roof, and the potential for conflict made for a volatile recipe!

As for Jacob, how was he to fill the role of father figure when the children knew he was *not* their father—and they missed their father. This created an extremely sticky situation for Jacob, one that clearly called for him to step up and provide wise, grandfatherly leadership.

The children clearly needed discipline that their mother was unable to provide at the time. This was no time for Jacob and Sara to back down. The futures of two precious grandchildren were on the line.

Little by little, the family fell into a routine. Jacob assumed the responsibilities of a father figure, which alone had a tremendously positive effect on the children. It gave them a much-needed sense of security when Grandpa was in charge.

Sara, well into her fifties at the time, learned to cope with two young grandchildren, ages two and four, during the long hours her daughter worked. In her heart, Sara was thankful to be available to help because she loved them all. It wasn't long, however, before major bumps loomed in the road.

By day, Sara was the disciplinarian while Jessica was at work. However, as soon as Mommy came home, the reins of parenting responsibility were passed back to her. Weary from a day's work and emotionally drained from her divorce, Jessica became passive in her parenting. She gave in to what the children wanted and ignored situations that called for parental leadership. This pattern made it especially difficult for Grandma. Each day, she had to undo the standard of permissive parenting from the previous evening and re-establish boundaries for the children's behavior. The children clearly struggled with the inconsistent standard between Mommy and Grandma.

The children clearly struggled with the inconsistent standard between Mommy and Grandma.

Jacob stepped in and spoke kindly but firmly to his daughter.

"Jessica, you can't expect your mother to discipline your children all day, and then you come home in the evening and undo it all. The children need some stability in their lives. We are going to have to devise a workable solution for the sake of the children."

Thankfully, they were all willing to sit down together and have a frank family discussion about the situation. In the end, they brainstormed several solutions.

Sara learned to call upon the loving authority of God's Word over her grandchildren. When problems arose, she led the children to her open Bible and said, "Let's see what your Father in heaven has to say about this matter." Then she pulled her grandchildren onto her lap and paraphrased a short, appropriate verse to them. In essence, God Himself became the Father figure and the ultimate "male" role model in the family. And through the reading of His Word, grace flowed into the children, even if they were too young to fully understand at the time.

Jacob, on the other hand, did not face the discipline hurdles that the women-folk had. His masculine presence in the room seemed to work magic. He took on the role of supporting his daughter's authority in her family by stepping in as needed and saying to the children, "You children need to do what your mother has told you to do." Each night at bedtime, Jacob laid his hands on the children's heads and prayed a blessing over them. With a kiss and a hug from Sara, the children ended each day on a peaceful note.

When problems arose, she led the children to her open Bible and said, "Let's see what your Father in heaven has to say about this matter."

Jacob and Sara were intentional in demonstrating their affection for one another in front of their grandchildren, knowing the children had been deprived of seeing a strong marriage modeled in their own home. They knew it would leave a lasting impression on the children to have a front row view of the beautiful drama of love that flowed between Grandma and Grandpa. After work each night, Jacob rescued his wife from her strenuous day by taking her for a walk in the neighborhood. One weekend a month, he took her away from the bustling household for an overnight "date." Sara loved the pleasant anticipation of these dates. They rejuvenated her energy, and they afforded Jessica some valuable *alone time* with her children as well.

Jacob and Sara's story had a happy ending. After six years, Jessica remarried a kind, godly man. Jacob and Sara were now free to be *just* the grandparents. The whole family was grateful to the Lord for providing grace and wisdom when it was most needed.

THOUGHTS TO PONDER

The Lord knows all about relational pain and betrayal in families. From Adam and Eve's disobedience to Him in the garden of Eden, to the children of Israel turning from Him over and over again, to His own Son being despised, rejected, and crucified by those He came to save, history is filled with stories of betrayal by those the Lord loves. He understands our human pain. And He has called us as grandparents to be instruments of healing and pillars of strength in our families, as much as it is possible for us.

No matter how many years of life you have traveled behind you, as you look forward through the dashboard window, be encouraged that God is still about the business of changing families that are train wrecks into families that follow Christ. No matter how old you are, it is never too late for the future legacy of your family to begin with your small footprints of faith.

He has called us as grandparents to be instruments of healing and pillars of strength in our families, as much as it is possible for us.

At the same time, it is a delicate line we walk when it comes to engaging in the discipline of our grandchildren. All the yellow warning lights flash: *potential danger zone ahead!* In this zone, our most valuable role is to support our grown children in their parenting—not interfere with or undermine their efforts. We can be active, not passive, in supporting the parents. We can lead our grandchildren to the Word of God and let them be *taught by the Lord.* We can pray for and trust in the Lord's promise: "Great shall be the peace of your children."

As a concluding reminder: we are not the parents—we are the *grandparents*. It is our season to step aside and let the parents be the parents.

OUR PRAYER

Our Father, who art in heaven,

How amazing it is that, no matter how old we grow, You are still a Father to us. We can always come to You when we are in need of wisdom and grace for the day.

"Ask, and it will be given to you; seek, and you will find; knock, and it will be opened to you. For everyone who asks receives, and he who seeks finds, and to him who knocks it will be opened.... If you then, ... know how to give good gifts to your children, how much more will your Father who is in heaven give good things to those who ask Him!" *(Matthew 7:7–11).*

Lord, may You give us soft hearts toward our family members, especially those who stray from You. May You give us opportunities to invest in the people who matter most to us and time to invest in them. May You give us wisdom that is just right for each unique situation, and may You give us strength to persevere in faithful service to those You have called us to.

We come to You as a Father and ask for all these things in Jesus' name. We know You will never turn us away empty-handed.

Amen.

12 • A CALL TO GRANDFATHERS: LIVING AND LEADING AS PATRIARCHS

You shall love the LORD your God with all your heart, with all your soul, and with all your strength. And these words which I command you today shall be in your heart. You shall teach them diligently to your children, and shall talk of them when you sit in your house, when you walk by the way, when you lie down, and when you rise up.

—Deuteronomy 6:5–7

When I picture a *patriarch*, I imagine the stereotypical images from greeting cards and animated movies: *images of ancient men with flowing white beards, wizened with age, sitting atop remote mountains, bestowing words of extraordinary wisdom upon all who will take heed.*

I am about to dispel that mythical picture! Being a patriarch is not quite like it is depicted on greeting cards or in movies. More realistically, patriarchs are flesh and blood, ordinary men with faults and foibles, just like everyone else. Just because we live to see many birthdays, does not mean that we have answers for all the family's problems! However, I believe that, if we seek the Lord for answers, He does grant us wisdom that is just right for our families.

From ancient times, a patriarch was simply the reigning head, or eldest male member, of a family unit. Sometimes, though, I think we men are better described by the Middle English derivative of *husband*: meaning a "house boor," or boor of the household! In any case, contrary to the image of a patriarch sitting in isolation on a mountaintop, we are called to be integrally involved with our families—something that does not come naturally for many of us men who would be content to dwell in man-caves!

As I turn eighty years old this year, I have a long life over which to reflect. I have more than enough memories to both laugh over and cry over. I am not the man with all the answers. To be honest, it has been difficult for me to lead my family spiritually. On many occasions, I have needed Dottie to be my coach and chief motivator. She has been a faithful helpmate, as I have needed her to prod me like a sheep when I've been slow to step up to the plate and respond! Having not had the influence of strong male role models in my life during my formative growing years, I have often felt like the race started without me. I stepped up to the starting line quite late in life. However, we men are never disqualified from the race, no matter how late we start. I am no authority on what it means to live and lead as a patriarch; I am simply a work-in-progress, limping along the journey to the finish line, with a prevailing passion to finish the race strong. From my own shattered roots, to the position of patriarch of four living generations, I am deeply indebted to the God who has redeemed me from my past and holds my future in His hands.

> **If we men fail to put on the cloak of leadership, what will come upon the generations that follow us?**

If we men fail to wear the cloak of leadership, what will come upon the generations that follow us? If we fail to take up the mantle of a patriarch, whose influence will our sons and grandsons give themselves over to? What will happen if the role of a family patriarch becomes lost with our generation? Regrettably, the idea of a man assuming the responsibilities of a patriarch and leading his family well is fast disappearing from our culture. Men whose lives exemplify this ideal are becoming even more rare.

Think back on earlier generations when it was normal for fathers to teach their sons a trade or to apprentice other young men in a vocation. If men had relinquished that role, countless valuable skills might have been lost. Likewise, if we men do not mentor the next genera-

Godly leadership does not mean domination or authoritarian control.

tion and speak of what it means to lead as godly patriarchs, as we *sit in our homes, walk by the way, lie down, and rise up* (Deuteronomy 6:7), we will lose a treasure of supreme value. We cannot afford to be passive in this, thereby allowing this treasure of a patriarchy to become lost! We *need* men in these times who will rise to the challenge; lead their families well; stand as encouragers to other men; serve as models and mentors to a new generation of young men; and initiate godly male leadership.

WHAT DOES IT MEAN TO LEAD AS A PATRIARCH?

As a male, I tend to focus on what is practical and rational. (I need Dottie to function as my better half when it comes to emotional sensitivity!) Few concepts have been as misinterpreted or misused throughout history as that of male leadership or biblical "headship." Other men whose credentials far outweigh my own have already written much on this topic. I want to emphasize here that godly leadership does *not* mean domination or authoritarian control. It does *not* mean steamrolling over the needs and feelings of others in an authoritarian manner.

What follows are some practical thoughts on what godly male leadership *does* look like. I share here some of the attributes of a patriarch that I have learned from others and from God's Word over the years—qualities that have yielded blessings in my own family.

- Perhaps first and foremost, being a godly patriarch means loving and cherishing one's wife while she is living. A leader is called to warmly and selflessly care for his wife—and do it openly, where the children can see and learn that it is a good thing! *"Husbands, love your wives, just as Christ also loved the church and gave Himself for her, . . . let each one of you in particular so love his own wife as himself"* (Ephesians 5:25–33).

Being a godly patriarch means loving and cherishing one's wife while she is living.

- Being a leader grants us men a *platform to serve* those under our care. We are responsible to meet the needs of our families and protect those under our care. Wives can be of great help to their husbands in this role. I remember one occasion when our daughters were young. I was standing outside our old car, drenched in the pouring rain, inflating the tires, while Dottie was inside the car prompting our girls, "See how Daddy is taking care of us? That is how God takes care of us!"

- Tell your children and grandchildren stories of how the Lord God has worked in miraculous ways—both in your life personally and in history. Most children never tire of hearing stories. Stories are an inoffensive way to plant memorable seeds of truth in their hearts. Delving even deeper, our children and grandchildren, for the most part, belong to a generation that does not personally know the horrors of war or persecution or severe deprivation. They need to know what it is like to cry out to God in desperate need of Him, and to see Him respond in miraculous ways. We can share with them stories of such times.

- Let your children and grandchildren see you loving God passionately. Living a life of dry obedience to the Lord will not impact a child's life nearly as much as seeing you live for the Lord and speak of His ways *passionately. That* will leave a lasting impression on them.

- Speak often to the members of your household of God's great love for them.

- Pray over your grandchildren, at mealtimes, at bedtimes, and in private. You have them as a captive audience at mealtimes, while bedtime has a way of opening windows to a child's heart. Even the most aloof child often begins to chatter away as he or she is being tucked in at night.

Living a life of dry obedience to the Lord will not impact a child's life nearly as much as seeing you live for the Lord and speak of His ways passionately.

- Confess your own failures to your children and grandchildren. Apologize when appropriate and ask their forgiveness. Few things are more effective in imparting healing to a family. *"God resists the proud, but gives grace to the humble"* (1 Peter 5:5).

- Share fun experiences with your grandchildren as often as possible. They point to the lovingkindness of the Lord without preaching a sermon. Outdoor experiences can be especially effective for displaying the greatness of the Lord to children of all ages.

- An interesting discovery I have made over the years is that many males are visual learners. That means we need pictures to help us grasp concepts! So buy a picture Bible for your grandsons and lead them through it together. You are never too old to enjoy a few pictures yourself!

- We can demonstrate an attitude of sincere interest in the life of each grandchild. We can ask questions and learn to be active listeners. For example,

Asking probing questions requires skill and tact, as we certainly do not want to be viewed as meddling grandparents!

"I hear you got a new snowboard. I don't think I'll try it, but I'd love to go out with you and watch you practice your moves!"

"I'm proud of you for making the soccer team this season. Mind if I come to your game on Saturday?"

"Are you learning to read this year? How about if you read me a story?"

Sometimes taking an interest in a grandchild's life means tactfully offering the wisdom of our years. As they grow older, we can challenge them with questions that diplomatically guide them to make wise choices. For example,

"That sure is a great-looking car. Let's look up safety features together and create a list of operating expenses."

"I agree with you. She is beautiful. What do you know about her values or her inner heart beauty?"

Asking probing questions requires skill and tact, as we certainly do not want to be viewed as meddling grandparents!

- We can make ourselves available to help when needs arise. Imagine what a tremendous show of trust it would be to say to a grandchild who has proven himself to be responsible, "Would you like to borrow my car to drive your date to the prom?" That is something a grandson would never forget!

- As patriarchs, we can give our grown children the freedom to make decisions with their own families, for the good of *their* families. We need to resist the temptation to register disapproval when our grown children don't do what *we* think they ought to do. This is *their* season to grow together as a couple and as a family. This is their season under God to leave their father and mother (emotionally) and be joined to one another (Genesis 2:24).

There is a time for young fledglings to spread their wings and fly from the nest. As patriarchs, we can offer our experienced arms to shield our children from a free fall. We can offer our support at times when our grown children need us. Our role did not end when our children turned eighteen; our role just looks different in this season of life. We are no longer calling in every shot; we are offering our support when needed.

> **As patriarchs, we can give our grown children the freedom to make decisions with their own families, for the good of their families.**

- One of the most meaningful and enduring gifts we can offer our young people is the gift of speaking openly about our impending mortality. How few of us in our western culture speak freely and comfortably about the eventual end of our lives on earth. We often speak of such things in hushed tones, away from the ears of children; yet crossing the threshold to the other side of eternity is the unalterable reality for every single one of us. As grandparents, we are in the winter season of our lives, living closer to eternity every day. What a glorious sermon our lives would preach to our precious young spectators if they were to observe our inner peace and hear our eager anticipation as we speak of the eternal glories that await us! Through our example, we can be a powerful influence in calming one of a child's greatest fears and inspiring those who will one day follow our footsteps into eternity.

- Lastly, if you are a first generation believer in the Lord and a pioneer of faith in your family, you can turn the tide of your entire family. *You are called by God to rise up as a leader of faith in your family.* God will help you. God will teach you. God will equip you!

DISPELLING DOUBTS AND OBJECTIONS

What follows are some of the most common objections I have heard from men who shy away from donning the cloak of leadership and accepting the responsibilities of a patriarch in their families.

- *"I'm exhausted after a day of work. When I come home, I just want to relax and unwind."*

If you are a first generation believer in the Lord and a pioneer of faith in your family, you can turn the tide of your entire family.

We all need to unwind when we transition from the working world to family life. Go ahead and de-stress when you first come home—whether you take a walk or spend a few minutes in solitude—but put a time limit on it. Then jump in and serve your family. Their appreciation will make it well worth whatever you sacrificed!

- *"I'm older. My children are older. We have had established role patterns in our home for years. Isn't it too late to change?"*

It is never too late to change! Change began in our family when I confessed that I had not done it all right. Talk to your grown children about it. Talk to your wife about it. Tell them your desires and your goal of being more involved with your children and grandchildren. Enlist their support as you step out and begin to shoulder the mantle of leadership in new ways.

A WORD OF ENCOURAGEMENT

Lastly, I would like to offer a word of encouragement to those women who are raising children or grandchildren in homes without male leadership. This is one of the greatest tragedies of our times. The shortage of worthy male role models in the home has become pandemic. If this is your situation, there is hope for your family. Turn to the Lord. Establish *Him* as the Patriarch of your family.

When you are in need of wisdom, or when you are in need of a partner in grandparenting, go before your heavenly Father and ask Him for all that you need.

> *But You have seen, for You observe trouble and grief,*
> *To repay it by Your hand.*
> *The helpless commits himself to You;*
> *You are the Helper of the fatherless* (Psalm 10:14).

The Lord Jesus is your Helper. He is your perfect Bridegroom. He is a Father to your children and a Patriarch to your grandchildren. When you are in need of wisdom, or when you are in need of a partner in grandparenting, go before your heavenly Father and ask Him for all that you need. Open God's Word together with your children and your grandchildren. Say to them, "Let's see what your Father in heaven has to say about this situation." He will never turn you away empty-handed!

THOUGHTS TO PONDER

There is a well-known story by an anonymous author about a wife who habitually cut off the ends of her hams before putting them into a roasting pan. For years, her husband watched her do this, pained by the waste of perfectly good meat as he watched her systematically chop off both ends of countless hams and throw them into the trash. But believing that his wife knew what she was doing in the kitchen, he never questioned this odd ritual. Finally, after many years, the husband finally could bear it no longer, and he questioned his wife, "Why do you do this strange thing?"

The man's wife was taken aback, having never actually paused to consider *"why?"* After pondering the question for several minutes, she replied, "I don't know why. I saw my mother do it, so I do it."

At that, the husband picked up the phone, called his mother-in-law, and asked, "Why do you cut off the ends of hams and throw them away?"

Children take in everything about us, and like it or not, they become imitators of us.

The man's mother-in-law answered, "Because I have a small roasting pan. That's the only way I can make hams fit in it."

Granted, this seems like a silly story, but it illustrates the point well. Many of us have picked up plenty of practices by observing our parents and grandparents—both irrational quirks and behaviors worthy of emulating. Likewise, we pass down plenty of life lessons to our children and grandchildren. Their eyes and ears are fixed on us, and they are soaking in our words and our actions—for the good and for the bad. Children take in everything about us, and like it or not, they become imitators of us. That alone is reason enough to justify taking our call to leadership as patriarchs solemnly.

Some of us inherited a legacy of painful memories from the patriarchs of our own families; some of us are currently living in painful situations. What hope is there for us?

As hard as this may be to hear, the place to begin is to *forgive* those who have let us down or wounded us. Then, God can begin to heal our hearts. We can begin to look at our circumstances through the lens of God's truth. God is a sovereign God. That means He was and is present in every circumstance of our lives. We can trust Him at His Word. One day, the Lord will wipe away every tear from our eyes (Revelation 21:4). *"And we know that all things work together for good to those who love God, to those who are the called according to His purpose"* (Romans 8:28).

> **God is a sovereign God. That means He was and is present in every circumstance of our lives.**

Finally, as grandparents and as patriarchs, we can resolve that we will be the ones to break the patterns of iniquity in our families. *We* will be the ones to pass down a new legacy—a legacy of faith-filled life and love. Take a moment to pause and let the power and significance of those resolutions sink in.

OUR PRAYER

Dear Lord,

Let us not shrink back from the role to which You have called us as men. Let us remember that it is You who has called us—and if You have called us, You will equip us. This is a call for us to walk closely with You, in obedience and surrender, for this calling to serve our families as godly leaders will cut across our natural tendencies and selfish desires. We will need Your grace, moment by moment. But the fruit of our surrendered lives will be greater than we can imagine, for there are generations at stake. Our influence on those who follow us is more far-reaching than our human eyes can see. Let us not take our calling to godly leadership lightly nor presume that someone else will carry the mantle for us. May we be remembered as men who walked with You and obeyed You all the days of our lives.

In Jesus' name,

Amen.

13 • SHARING GRANDCHILDREN WITH THE IN-LAWS

Do nothing out of selfish ambition or vain conceit. Rather, in humility value others above yourselves, not looking to your own interests but each of you to the interests of others. In your relationships with one another, have the same mindset as Christ Jesus.
—Philippians 2:3–5 NIV

Enfolded in a soft pink blanket with a pink cap hugging her head, our precious baby granddaughter was carried expertly by the nurse closer to the window. With our noses pressing up against the nursery window and our eyes beholding the most beautiful baby ever created, we shared similar thoughts with the woman standing next to us.

Ruth, the "other" mother-in-law, had arrived at the maternity ward window, just as we were leaving.

"My son's baby," she sighed.

"Our daughter's baby," we responded knowingly.

"Isn't she the most beautiful baby you have ever seen?" we both thought in unison.

DOTTIE SHARES...

Say the word *in-law* in public, and you invariably evoke a whole host of responses. From the subtle eye-roll that communicates, "Oh yeah, in-laws can be a pain," to coarse jokes, sitcom writers and comedians have earned a fortune at the expense of in-laws.

The truth is that in-laws can be one of God's greatest blessings to grandchildren. So why all the negative press surrounding in-laws? My guess is that it is a challenge to be in close relationship to any human being over the long haul, much less a relationship that is not of our choosing. We acquire in-laws by default; they come as a package deal with their child. Add in to the mix our human propensity toward jealousy and the power of jealousy to wreak havoc on relationships, and in-laws make for a potentially volatile family recipe.

I felt completely blindsided when the green-eyed monster attacked me in full force—in the person of a loving grandmother-in-law.

How different our secular world's ideas are from the Lord's design for family relationships. His Word tells us in Romans 12:10 NIV, *"Be devoted to one another in love. Honor one another above yourselves."* As one who is naturally drawn to people and is soft-wired for relationships, I was convinced I could fulfill that Scripture—until I was put to the test.

Seeing that precious, tiny child in the maternity nursery, our first grandchild, my heart did somersaults of love. Yet, that very state of enthralled love was the thing that made me most vulnerable to feelings of jealousy and hurt. Where that child was concerned, I was *extremely* vulnerable. It dawned on me with all the subtlety and gentleness of a brick that this was not *our* grandchild alone. There was another grandparent in the picture. And we were called to share with her. But how do you share a *baby?*

That is when the green-eyed monster named *Jealousy* reared its destructive head. I felt threatened by this lovely woman who stood next to me at the window, and terribly immature. Not one who is normally prone to jealousy, I felt completely blindsided when the green-eyed monster attacked me in full force—in the person of a loving grandmother-in-law. Pride gripped my heart. I wanted to be first in my grandchild's life. The fear of being replaced by another grandmother was emotionally overwhelming for me. An alarm triggered deep inside me: my first granddaughter might love her Nana more than her Mom-Mom. How much I had yet to learn.

The fear of being replaced by another grandmother was emotionally overwhelming for me.

The alienating sin of jealousy began to creep into my loyal friendship with Ruth and threatened to spoil our relationship. My friendship with Ruth and her late husband, Andy, traced back ten years to the time when our kids, Warren and Kimberly, were in junior high school together. Roger and I went to basketball games together with Ruth and Andy. By high school, Warren and Kim had become best friends, and by the time they were college sophomores, they were dating seriously. We were all thrilled with the budding romance and prayed that the Lord would unite our two children in marriage. One year later, he answered our prayer.

To me, Ruth was a sweet, wonderful, older woman of faith. She was twenty years older than I, although that never really mattered until our first grandchild came along. Baby Julie was a very special and timely gift to Ruth because Ruth had just lost her husband. Julie Dawn represented a gift of new life from the Lord.

REALITY SETS IN

While everything about being a grandmother was totally new to me, Ruth was an experienced pro. She had already had three grandchildren.

Thoughts spawned by jealousy began colliding in my brain. I felt like I was competing with Ruth rather than being blessed by her. After all, she lived almost around the corner from my granddaughter and had more time to spend with the baby. She was more available to help with meals and housework. Honestly, I did not know where I fit in to the picture—or if I even fit in at all. Ruth was doing it all so well.

Not only was Ruth bonding with our granddaughter, but what made matters worse, in *my* mind, was that she and my daughter were sharing so much quality time together. That didn't help my own relationship with my daughter. I felt like I was being compared to her mother-in-law, and I could never measure up. I felt insecure, confused, and hurt. I felt that my mother-in-law had replaced me in my daughter and granddaughter's lives. I missed the comfortable relationship I had shared with my daughter. The truth was, I had made the entire situation all about *me*. As I heaped slight upon slight, I sank deeper and deeper into the pit I was creating. One would think *I* was the one suffering from postpartum hormones!

Though I did not realize it at the time, I had allowed a silent wall of resentment to take shape in my heart.

As so often happens when self-absorbed thoughts are allowed to run wild, I had completely misunderstood the situation between my daughter, Kim, and her mother-in-law, Ruth. Kim was simply trying to honor her mother-in-law. She understood that Ruth was feeling the loss of recent widowhood, and she was sensitive to Ruth's need to be needed. While Ruth was still mourning the loss of her husband, Kim reached out to her and included her in the new life of a grandchild.

However, because I was so insecure about being replaced as a grandmother, I misinterpreted Kim's kindness in honoring her mother-in-law as rejection of me.

As time went on, I began to sense that there was something even bigger and more ominous taking root in my heart. A deep-seated seed of resentment was sprouting to life in my heart. *Where is that coming from?* I wondered. I could not blame it on Ruth or my daughter. It had nothing to do with either of them. And then memories began trickling back to me.

My own mother had been a dedicated schoolteacher who poured long hours into her students. That left little time for her to be a grandmother to our three daughters. There were times I longed for my mother's help. Though I did not realize it at the time, I had allowed a silent wall of resentment to take shape in my heart.

On the heels of jealousy and resentment, the companion sin of self-pity began nipping at my heels.

As I struggled with jealousy in my earliest years as a grandmother, buried streams of resentment also bubbled to the surface. They affected my relationship with my family, and most of all, they affected my relationship with the Lord. On the heels of jealousy and resentment, the companion sin of self-pity began nipping at my heels. I was not in a good place. I tried hard to plaster on a happy face, but on the inside, I was growing depressed. *Hey, wait a minute! Wasn't I a grown grandmother? Wasn't I too grown-up to be battling these child-like emotions?*

ANSWERED PRAYER

Depression is a dark and lonely place. I lived in a world that was all about me. I justified and buried the resentment and unforgiveness that were poisoning my heart. Finally, I felt so weighed down with conviction that I had to face the truth.

At first, the truth about myself was difficult to admit. I had been born again as a child of God. *Why wasn't it working?* My family was suffering. My marriage was suffering. I was not the kind of grandmother I had dreamed of being. I was stuck in a pit of despondency. I needed help!

The Lord provided help in the form of a godly older woman named Henrietta. Henrietta was also a grandmother. Having walked with the Lord for over thirty years, she was more mature in her faith than I. She graciously walked through this season alongside me. Henrietta understood the process of sanctification—how a person's life can be transformed into the image of Christ, often in the heat of trials—and she shared her wisdom with me at a time when I needed it most. She had a way of reaching back into her past and drawing forth memories of times the Lord had brought her through serious trials in her own faith. She shared these with me in a way that I understood. Even we grandparents need someone, at times, to come alongside us and steer us in the right direction!

The Lord provided help in the form of a godly older woman.

It seemed like it took forever before the jealousy monster released its suffocating hold on me. But Henrietta was patient and faithful to continue encouraging me from the Word of God, helping me to understand the role repentance and forgiveness play in the gospel.

As I began to repent of the jealousy and resentment long buried in my heart, I received God's forgiveness. I sensed that my heart was mysteriously softening, not only toward Ruth, but also toward my mother and others around me. My spiritual eyes opened to see the way I let my emotions rule me. Emotions are powerful; they have a mind of their own; and mine often misled me. I saw clearly that my sin of jealousy was a form of fear—fear of losing something that I valued. What I was grasping for was a special place in my daughter and granddaughter's lives. In response, I gave in to jealousy and resentment because I feared I would not get what I wanted. Ironically, I drove away the very thing I wanted most.

My problem was that I did not know *who I was in Christ*. I was insecure in my identity. The words of the apostle Paul cut through to my heart:

> *Brothers and sisters, I could not address you as people who live by the Spirit but as people who are still worldly—mere infants in Christ.... For since there is jealousy and quarreling among you, are you not worldly? Are you not acting like mere humans?* (1 Corinthians 3:1–3 NIV).

The light bulb flickered on at last, illuminating the truth. The person I once was—insecure, immature, envious—was now figuratively dead, having died in the crucifixion of Christ. I was now *alive*, a new creation in Christ! It

As my heart was reconciled to the Lord, everything else began to fall into place.

was high time I started to live like a new creation! Soon, my depression began to lift. God was transforming my heart and opening my eyes to see what I had been missing: God-honoring relationships with those around me. He replaced my jealousy of Ruth with respect for her. He also restored my relationship with my daughter and gave me my *own* relationship with my granddaughter. As my heart was reconciled to the Lord, everything else began to fall into place. Our extended family grew closer than ever.

My mother lived the last ten years of her life with Roger and me, where we had made a place for her in our home. Our final memories together were beautiful. Our children and grandchildren reaped the precious blessing of my fully restored relationship with my mother. With God's grace and through the power of forgiveness, I have been set free from the influences of past generations. God has changed me. The green-eyed monster of jealousy has been slain, and I rejoice with great joy as I grandparent in unity with our in-laws!

One of the things that I have most enjoyed has been the opportunity to encourage other grandmothers in their calling as grandparents. Listening to these dear ladies open up about their joys and their heartaches, I am amazed by how often similar scenarios play out in many of their homes. Names and details may be different. Personalities may also be different. But the common themes are the same. I would like to share four of these grandmotherly stories with you.

SALLY'S STORY . . .

It was a struggle for me when my son was newly married. My son and I have similar personalities, and we used to love spending time together in deep discussions. Adjusting to life without him has been difficult for me.

I love the wife my son chose. She is a dear girl, and I never wanted my hurt feelings to interfere with their marriage. However, sometimes I resented the time my son spent with her extended family. It felt like I had lost not only a son, but also my close friend.

A few years ago, grandchildren began to arrive. It seemed obvious to me that the other grandmother was favored. I was envious and felt like my heart was breaking. I was feeling completely shut out of the family picture. But what could I do? My husband suggested that we grandparents sit down together and openly discuss the matter. So we did.

What relief our discussion brought. My son's mother–in-law admitted she was completely in the dark. She had no idea how I had been feeling. She felt bad and assured me it had not been her intention to exclude me. She asked for my forgiveness, which I gladly gave her. I, too, asked her to forgive me for holding resentment rather than speaking up. God was so good! He brought forgiveness and healing in our relationship and in our extended family. It was a fresh reminder to me how often we misinterpret what the other person is really feeling, and how vital honest communication is in our relationships.

It was a fresh reminder to me how often we misinterpret what the other person is really feeling, and how vital honest communication is in our relationships.

Today, my husband and I have the freedom to be with our grandchildren often, and we play an important role in their lives. I have to give credit to my daughter-in-law's mother for the turn-around in our family. She had the maturity to humble herself and ask forgiveness, and in doing so, she became the catalyst that brought our family together.

CAROL'S STORY...

I have a sweet daughter-in-law who is a good wife to my son. Her mother, Betty, used to be outgoing and caring. We enjoyed lunches and shopping together and seemed to have a mutually accepting friendship. We had a rude awakening when our first grandchild was born. Everything changed. To me, it felt more like a nightmare.

Betty no longer wanted anything to do with me. She is quite close to her daughter, so when she was not working, she spent most of her time helping her daughter with the new baby. When I invited Betty to lunch or to join me shopping, she never seemed to have time for me. Because my daughter-in-law is a good wife to my son, I didn't want to interfere with their relationship. However, I did want to be involved in my grandson's life, and I wanted things to be like they once were with Betty. I was feeling the pain of rejection.

The dilemma was puzzling to me. How could I honor Betty as my son's mother-in-law when she shut me out of her life?

To be honest, I felt like telling Betty off, but I knew that wouldn't help the situation. Instead, I decided to write her a letter. After much thought and prayer, this is what I wrote:

Dear Betty,

The Lord has truly blessed us both with our grandchild, Kevin. I know that you and Howard love our grandson as much as Jim and I do.

I'm grateful for your continued support for your daughter. I understand that a daughter's relationship is closer to her mother than to her mother-in-law. I adore your daughter. She is the perfect wife for Robert. I want to thank you for raising her to be a wonderful mother for our grandchild.

I miss our luncheons at the Tea Room and shopping at the Mall. I know you are busy helping your daughter, but as her mother-in-law and Kevin's grandmother, I would love to spend some time together with them and with you. Perhaps you could arrange this for me? I am free next Tuesday or Wednesday afternoon.

Love,
Carol

Betty and I did get together, and to my surprise, my daughter-in-law asked me if I would consider babysitting Kevin in the fall. She had to return to work and needed someone to care for him during the day. Since Betty also worked, I was the only one available to fill this role. I jumped at the opportunity. I have my grandson from seven in the morning till two every afternoon. I'm so glad that I slowed down, regained control over my emotions, and took the time to pray. It helped me to show Betty respect and not tell her off. Believe me, I was tempted. The Lord has His ways of making things right when we submit our plans to Him.

MARIANNE'S STORY...

We were happy when our daughter, Mary, married Mark. He seemed like a wonderful man. They were the perfect couple, or so we thought. Even though we didn't know Mark's parents, we trusted Mary's judgment. After all, they were to be her in-laws, not ours. We never anticipated that they would be a problem until our first grandchild entered into the family.

Once Mark and Mary announced that she was expecting, his parents completely took over. They immediately bought everything a baby could need. There certainly was no need for me to throw my daughter a baby shower. Thoughts raged inside me, like, *Hey, I'm the other grandmother. Don't I fit in here?* I felt unneeded and helpless.

> **The Lord has His ways of making things right when we submit our plans to Him.**

I tried speaking up, but Mark's mother's ears were deaf to my appeals. She was in a world all her own. Mark and Mary tried talking to his parents, but to no avail. His mother was in control.

After the baby arrived, things grew worse. I was completely left out of my daughter's life and my new granddaughter Rachel's life. Dealing with her strong-willed mother-in-law left my daughter feeling defeated. She felt like she was in a vise, trapped between two grandmothers fighting over her baby.

After enduring two months of this, Mark stepped in. To protect his wife and save his marriage, he ordered his mother to stay away. Then, to keep peace in the family, Mark and Mary decided it would be best for neither grandparent to have access to Rachel. Needless to say, I was heartbroken.

Today, Rachel is three years old and has a little sister, whom we've never seen. My daughter and her family have moved across the country. My relationship with my daughter is greatly strained, and I've given up hope of ever having a relationship with my grandchildren.

As I think back over all that has transpired in our family, there are many things I should have done differently. I should not have made such an issue over my feelings being hurt, and my needs not being met. I could have spoken up in kindness—and then let it go and been patient, allowing everyone to adjust to a new baby in the family. I should not have put my daughter in the middle between two feuding grandmothers. Instead, I could have shown thankfulness to the other grandparents for their generosity. I should have swallowed my pride and hurt feelings and continued to reach out in love to others. I have paid a heavy price for putting my own feelings and resentments at the forefront of everything. My two grandchildren don't even know me, and I have no opportunity to change that. I often ask myself, "Was it worth it?"

> **While a man needs his independence as he learns to lead his new family, a daughter needs her mother's experience.**

What a contrast between Carol's story and Marianne's story—and what different outcomes each grandmother experienced.

While a man needs his independence as he learns to lead his new family, a daughter needs her mother's experience. My friend Karen shares her story.

KAREN'S STORY...

Our children's marriage was a joyful time for both families. Our children had known each other from childhood, and both families were delighted over the prospect of becoming in-laws—until the day our first grandchild was born. Almost overnight, both our relationship and our joy turned sour. The bond between our two families was broken, and so were our hearts. Where had we gone wrong?

When the baby came, I saw that our daughter-in-law preferred only her mother. Having only sons, I did not understand that special bond between a mother and daughter. Feeling rejected, I chose to withdraw and, sadly, missed the early days of my grandson's life.

My failure with our first grandbaby drove a wedge between families, and I was determined not to let this happen again. By the time our second grandchild was born, I had learned a most valuable lesson. I was not being rejected. Wanting one's mother is normal for a daughter in the seasons of life when she is adapting to her own role as a mother herself. I had to learn to step aside graciously and give my daughter-in-law the time and space that she needed.

Opening my Bible, I read the Lord's gentle reminder to make every effort to do what leads to peace (Romans 14:19).

My husband and I also discovered that we had not prepared our son adequately to lead his wife through this challenging time. Between two strongly opinionated grandmothers, our daughter-in-law was feeling emotionally overwhelmed, and our son was finding it difficult to maintain his position of leadership in his own home. Something had to change. That something was me.

Opening my Bible, I read the Lord's gentle reminder to make every effort to do what leads to peace (Romans 14:19). I pray that I will be able to help others not make the same mistakes I did. In the meantime, I know that God will help me to make up for lost time with my first grandson.

HONORING THE IN-LAWS

Once I was reconciled to Ruth, I was free to show her the honor to which she was due. My first step was to understand the unique relationship that exists between a mother and her son.

There is a saying that goes like this,

A son is a son
until he takes a wife,
but a daughter is a daughter
for the rest of her life.

Having raised only daughters, I was aware of how natural it is for a daughter to gravitate to her own mother. It was not until Kim married Warren that I discovered how very different the relationships are between a mother and *daughter*, and a mother and *son*. Neither had it occurred to me how the mother of a son might feel when he marries.

When a son marries, the child a mother has raised leaves her to be joined to another woman. All the years a mother has invested in training and caring for her son, wondering if he will ever learn to keep his room clean and worrying when he comes home late or doesn't call home, are displaced overnight. It is all according to God's plan—so it is a good thing. Her son has left her to join his life to his wife's.

For this reason a man shall leave his mother and be joined to his wife (Matthew 19:5).

A mother's singular vision, passion, and toil in raising her son to become a man are now in the hands of another woman. She has fulfilled her part. The mother of a son is called to fully release his future to his wife and to the Lord. It has been eye-opening for me to see and understand the feelings that a mother experiences when her son marries. Releasing one's son to a wife is not an easy thing for a mother to do, and it caused me to appreciate Ruth even more.

By the time our next two daughters, Robin and Lisa, were married and had children, my heart was in a totally different place. God had done a deep and gracious work of healing in me. I now understood the importance of honoring our in-laws for the sake of the grandchildren. Children need to know that they are free to build relationships with both sets of grandparents, and that their parents are supportive of this. Unity in the family is a precious gift to a grandchild. It's our calling as grandparents to be the leaders in love and leave a legacy of peace to our grandchildren.

As a way of honoring our in-laws, we include them in our family vacations and holiday dinners. We look for opportunities to share with them regularly our deep appreciation for all the years they spent raising their sons to be the men they are today.

Children need to know that they are free to build relationships with both sets of grandparents, and that their parents are supportive of this.

Our daughters also look for opportunities to honor their in-laws. For several years, one of our daughters gave her mother-in-law a bouquet of roses on her husband's birthday, along with a card thanking her for raising her son to be a responsible husband and a good father. All our girls give their in-laws open invitations to attend family birthday parties and holidays. It is a blessing to see our daughters passing on to their children the legacy of honoring their in-laws. Together we are family.

THOUGHTS TO PONDER

My human nature has certainly wanted its own way over the years! Left unchecked, I have wanted to be in control and have things done my way. The Lord has been so patient in teaching me time and time again that the only way to really *live* is to be *willing to die.* This death is a figurative death in which the Lord calls us to be willing to surrender our own way. We are called to live by the Spirit (Romans 8:14) and to relinquish those vestiges of selfish desire that lurk in our hearts. Thanks be to God! He has set me free from the need to pursue my own agenda! *"For the law of the Spirit of life in Christ Jesus has made me free from the law of sin and death"* (Romans 8:2).

In our role as grandparents, we have countless opportunities to live by the Spirit of God, rather than the law of human desire.

In our role as grandparents, we have countless opportunities to live by the Spirit of God, rather than the law of human desire. We can model this in our families every time we choose to put the well-being of others ahead of our own needs, convenience, or comfort. We can quietly "die" on the inside—leaving us free to serve the needs of others selflessly. What a legacy *that* would be to pass down through the generations!

Be encouraged that for whatever you give up in the present moment for the sake of serving others or bringing peace to your family, you will gain an infinitely greater reward for years and generations to come! The seeds of the Spirit that you sow now will be reaped a hundredfold in the future.

OUR PRAYER

Dear heavenly Father,

Search my heart and know me. Show me if there is any sinful or selfish way in me that displeases You and keeps me from loving our in-laws or setting a godly example for our grandchildren. I do not want my sin to hinder any of my grandchildren from knowing

You, nor do I want to hinder them from the benefit of having two diverse sets of grandparents. Forgive me for the times I did not understand or consider the feelings of our in-laws.

Thank you for Your kindness that has brought me to repentance. Your forgiveness is such a gracious gift to us, and I am so thankful for it.

I ask You to bless my relationships with our in-laws for the sake of unity in our families, for my grandchildren, and for Your glory. Give me divine inspiration for ways to show them the honor to which they are due.

In the name of Jesus,

Amen.

14 · SERVING OUR GROWN CHILDREN: BUILDING BRIDGES TO GRANDCHILDREN

But whoever desires to become great among you, let him be your servant. . . . just as the Son of Man did not come to be served, but to serve.

—Matthew 20:26–28

While I was preoccupied with discovering where I fit in with my grandmother-in-law Ruth, I unwittingly withdrew from Warren and Kim during their first weeks as new parents. Needless to say, this affected them. Pulling back was a knee-jerk response on my part, but what it lacked was sensitivity to Warren and Kim's needs.

Not wanting to intrude into the new little family's life together, Roger and I retreated to the comfortable back seats. We stayed away and waited to be invited back in. At the time, we thought it was the right thing to do. We came to understand that, to the contrary, we had made a big mistake. We were guilty of contributing to an uncomfortable communication breakdown.

Why aren't Kim and Warren calling us? I fretted. *Don't they know we are grandparents?? Don't they know we're supposed to be helpful, sup-*

portive, and involved? Kim and I had grown accustomed to talking on the phone at least once a week before she became a mother. Why not now? It was puzzling. *Where had we gone wrong?* We prematurely came to the unilateral conclusion that Kim and Warren simply did not need our help. At the same time, Roger and I could not shake off the itching desire to experience the miracle of new life together with them and grow to know our grandchild. *Lord, how do we DO this grandparenting thing?*

A week passed. Finally, the phone rang, and I heard a familiar voice on the other end. It was Kim.

"Mom, I miss you."

"I miss you, too, honey."

"Why haven't you called me, Mom?"

"I was afraid you would think I was interfering, so I waited for *you* to call *me.*"

"Seriously, Mom, that's something you don't ever need to worry about. You're not interfering at all."

Bam. It hit me that I had given myself over to an insecure fallacy all along.

A few minutes of honest communication was all it took to clear the air of our misunderstanding.

Isn't it ironic how ready we can be to presume that we know what another person is thinking—only to discover that they actually are not thinking that at all? A few minutes of honest communication was all it took to clear the air of our misunderstanding. Kimberly had felt awkward asking for help, and I had not wanted to appear presumptuous. Meanwhile, the reality was that we both needed one another at the time—and precious time with our granddaughter was ticking away!

The remedy was so simple and straightforward. I had merely complicated it into a tortuous muddle. If only I had been willing to step out and take the lead in calling Kim and Warren. I could have confessed honestly my fear of intruding, but then simply asked if they needed my help. Instead, I presumed wrongly what they were thinking and took the easier path of withdrawing.

That was the first, and one of the most significant, lessons we learned about serving our adult children: Serving means stepping out and taking initiatives, and *that* involves taking risks. But that is what love does—love takes risks for the good of the beloved. If we grandparents miss opportunities to serve our grown children, we miss priceless opportunities to build bridges to our grandchildren.

Ever since that first misunderstanding with Kim, we have looked for opportunities to serve our adult children. We never have to look very hard!

A rare treat for many young parents is time to spend alone together investing in their marriage. Roger and I relished opportunities to have our grandchildren come for sleepovers while their parents enjoyed some needed alone time. Somehow, the world looked a bit rosier when they came back refreshed!

Serving means stepping out and taking initiatives, and that involves taking risks.

At our house, the children knew where the toys, books, and activities were kept for a night of fun. With Mom-Mom and Pop-Pop in charge, a typical evening's itinerary might be pizza, ice cream, hide-and-seek, and an abundance of stories, culminating in the *pièce de résistance*—a special, late bedtime! When the children were younger, I made a little bed right beside our bed as a cozy place for the children to sleep. When they awoke in the morning, they crowded into bed with us before Roger had to leave for work.

What began as our way of serving our grown children ended up building strong, lasting bridges to our grandchildren. We still don't know who enjoyed these times more—the children, or us!

SERVING FROM A DISTANCE

When families are separated by distance, opportunities to serve them cannot realistically materialize as frequently or as spontaneously as we would like. Even so, we can still think ahead and make plans to spend quality alone time with our grandchildren as often as we can pull it off. Concocting our plans is half the fun! Though the times may be far between, planning for them gives everyone something tangible to anticipate.

When our children lived far away, serving them often meant jumping into the car and driving to *them*. Life was too short to be troubled over not seeing the grandchildren. It was *our* season to travel to them. Even though Roger was still working, our season of life did afford us greater flexibility than many young families with children have. For us, demonstrating a servant's heart meant being willing to trek to where the children were.

When our children lived far away, serving them often meant jumping into the car and driving to them.

Our youngest daughter, Lisa, and her husband, Doug, lived three hours away. When their first baby was due, I made arrangements to spend a week with them before the baby was born, helping Lisa to prepare the homecoming nest in that anxious, endless final week of waiting. How exciting it was to be present with them at the birth of their first baby! While Doug was at his wife's side, holding her hand, I paced and prayed quietly in the back of the room. I will never forget that experience. What a miracle it was!

Although the three-hour distance made it a bit of a stretch to stop in for a coffee chat or to help fold laundry, we still looked for ways and means to serve Doug and Lisa. Occasionally, Roger and I planned a weekend drive down to care for the children while Doug and Lisa relished an overnight getaway. What fun it was to play games together with their kids, watch videos, play in the park, and hike in the nearby woods. The finishing touch to our weekends was a glorious pilgrimage to the local dollar store with the four grandchildren. They always delighted us by insisting that we buy a gift for Mommy and Daddy, too, to greet them upon their return home. God bless the one who invented dollar stores!

After many years of traveling the distance to spend time with Doug and Lisa's family, we were elated when they moved back to Pennsylvania. In fact, Roger and I now live together *with* them! With Kim and Robin's families living nearby as well, we have all three of our daughters, their husbands, and *twenty-nine* grandchildren and great-grandchildren living close by. It's a grandparent's dream come true! While it may be a recipe for potential chaos, it affords us all abundant opportunities to serve one another!

> **It's only in hindsight that I now see more clearly the high calling of serving the next generations in my own family that I missed.**

MISSED OPPORTUNITIES TO SERVE

As our family has grown, and I reflect over the years, I am painfully aware of opportunities to serve my children that I missed. Granted, I spent my early years after our daughters were grown serving our church family and others in various capacities. However, in immersing myself in those *good* things, I question whether I missed out on doing some *better* things. There were opportunities to serve right in front of me that I did not even recognize at the time. It's only in hindsight that I now see more clearly the high calling of serving the next generations in my own family that I missed. I share some of these times here, in hopes that they will be an encouragement to other grandparents.

I missed one of my greatest opportunities to serve when Warren and Kim made the purposeful decision to homeschool their four children. It did not occur to me at the time how much help I could have been, considering the tremendous investment of time Kim was pouring into her children's educations.

Kimberly never asked me for help. Again, I made the mistake of assuming that she was doing just fine. I wish I had been more sensitive to her needs and more thoughtful by taking the initiative to reach out and offer to help with housework, ironing, grocery shopping, reading with the children—or any one of a dozen things I could have done to serve their family.

I could have offered to do the same for our middle daughter, Robin. Her young children kept her days full of activity, and I know she would have benefited from more help from Mom-Mom.

I missed valuable occasions to build bridges into their lives by serving their mothers.

By helping my daughters more, my grandchildren would have seen how much I cared. Golden opportunities abounded for me to model genuine servanthood before their young, observant eyes. I missed valuable occasions to build bridges into their lives by serving their mothers.

Today, thirty years later, Kim and Warren and Robin and Mike are grandparents themselves. Their servant hearts have displayed living examples of the way the Lord redeems generations. Their doors are always open for *their* daughters and daughters-in-law to drop off their children. If one of them has a sleepless night tending to a sick child or has a doctor's appointment or needs to go grocery shopping, Grandma Kim and Grandma Robin are available to help, while Grandpas Warren and Mike form the supporting cast!

Kim hosts "cousins' playtime" in her home, so the grandchildren can grow up together. Her spare bedroom has become a child's paradise with dolls and dress-up clothes and a miniature kitchen, most of which Kim salvaged from neighborhood yard sales.

Frequently, Robin can be found busy in her kitchen, cooking for her grandchildren's families. To give her daughter and daughter-in-law a night off from cooking, Robin has a special tradition of preparing dinners for their families along with her own. As a grandmother, she has the availability to put together a home-cooked meal for each of their families. When the girls come over to pick up Robin's dinners, she takes advantage of the opportunity to catch up on their family news.

One day, I commented to Kim wistfully, "You are a much better mom and grandmom than I ever was."

He will equip us to accomplish this good work that He has called us to.

Kim's response caught me off guard. "Don't you *want* it to be that way, Mom?" she asked gently.

I had to contemplate that for a moment. "That *is* how I want it. Yes, honey, I *do* want it to be that way." I want my daughters to surpass me. In turn, I want my grandchildren to reap the benefit of *their* parents' investments into them. Such is the awesome mystery and wonderful blessing of a family legacy. Each generation benefits from the previous generation, and their children after them are blessed to the third and fourth generations. That is God's design for families. He *will* equip us to accomplish this good work that He has called us to.

THOUGHTS TO PONDER

Children are like sponges. They soak in everything around them and tuck it all away in their hearts. It becomes part of who they are, and who they will grow up to become. Childhood memories are profoundly powerful. Imagine the impact we could have on our families by setting an example of serving one another across the generations!

OUR PRAYER

Dear heavenly Father,

By stepping back and looking through Your eyes, I can see how important it is to serve our married children and build bridges to our grandchildren. Having been a parent for so many years, my eyes simply were not focused to view things through a grandparent's glasses. Therefore, I missed many opportunities as a grandparent. Help me not to dwell on the past, but to start each new day with fresh grace from You. You are a God who redeems what the locust has eaten. Your mercies are new every morning. Your riches will make up for my poverty.

Lord, I need Your help daily to walk in the role to which You have called me. I so desire to serve wherever I am needed. Please remove any obstacles that hinder my relationships with my children and grandchildren. May I hear your gentle, quiet voice, and may I have the humility to respond and change when needed.

I ask You for Your blessing,

In Jesus' name.

Amen.

15 • SURROGATE GRANDPARENTS: A MATCH MADE IN HEAVEN

Serve one another humbly in love.

—Galatians 5:13 NIV

E ven as we write the words on these pages, we are painfully aware that there are many homes where one or both grandparents are absent from children's lives. Perhaps the void has been caused by the death of a grandparent. Perhaps the dissolution of a marriage has created a chasm between children and grandparents. Adult children may be estranged from their own parents for countless and varied reasons, with the result being that grandchildren are left without grandparents in their lives. Sometimes, there never was a lasting commitment between parents, leaving grandparents out of the family picture altogether. For others, geographic distance or physical infirmity keeps grandparents from their grandchildren, though their hearts may long to be close.

Not every absentee grandparent is the result of a negative circumstance. For example, the miles separating missionaries from their extended families are vast. Whatever the reason, the void that children feel when grandparents are not present in their lives may be sensitive and sore. It is to these families that we devote this chapter.

For children whose grandparents are absent from their lives, "surrogate grandparents" can appear like angels sent from heaven!

A *surrogate* is simply one who substitutes for another. In the case of grandparents, a surrogate may not necessarily *replace* the real grandparent. Rather, a surrogate may temporarily fill the void left by an absent grandparent. Wherever grandparents are missing, there is undoubtedly a need for a loving substitute to fill the emptiness. While God Himself is an ever-present help in time of need, there is also truth in the saying, "For hugging, you need the real thing." Real, flesh-and-blood hugs from a surrogate grandparent can feel indescribably comforting!

> **Wherever grandparents are missing, there is undoubtedly a need for a loving substitute to fill the emptiness.**

If you are a member of the "older" generation with some time and love to spare, this challenge may be for you. If you are a single man or woman, you may make a delightful "aunt" or "uncle" or surrogate grandparent to some precious child. There are children who need your love and attention. It does not take much sowing to reap bountiful rewards! There is something about a relationship between the generations that generates a blessing all the way around.

GWEN'S STORY...

There are times in life when grandparents can be a lifeline, but other times when the lifeline is not quite long enough to reach a family that is sinking. Gwen found herself in just such a situation. Her husband left her with three children. She was forced to find a job outside the home that would provide for her children. The dilemma was that daycare for three children would have cost half Gwen's income, making it an unrealistic option. Neither grandmother was available to help with childcare since they, too, worked.

Into the picture entered an "angel" named Audrey. Audrey was a widow in her sixties, who lived in Gwen's neighborhood. When Audrey learned of Gwen's predicament, she graciously volunteered to help with the children. She converted one room in her home into an inviting after-school play area for the children. Audrey quickly endeared herself to the children, who soon began calling her "Grandma Audrey."

At the end of the school day, the three children rushed to Grandma Audrey's home, where fresh baked cookies and other snacks were invariably waiting. She sat down with them as they munched and talked to them about their school days. After unwinding with a brief video time, Audrey had the children start on their homework until Gwen arrived. There were many nights that Audrey had dinner already prepared by the time Gwen came to pick up the children. This thoughtful gesture freed Gwen to spend some quality time with her children after a long day at work.

Look around—there are children everywhere who are missing one or both grandparents.

Knowing that money was scarce for Gwen, Audrey refused payment for watching the children. In return, Gwen cleaned Audrey's house every two weeks and helped her with her grocery shopping.

The love that Audrey showered on the children was reciprocated. She reaped as much joy *from* them as she gave *to* them. Her own grandchildren lived six hours away, and since her husband's death, she had not felt comfortable driving the long distance alone. Nurturing her three "adopted" little ones satisfied a longing in her own heart, in addition to blessing Gwen and the children in a way they could never repay.

THOUGHTS TO PONDER

Look around—there are children everywhere who are missing one or both grandparents. Seek the Lord's will regarding whether there is a child or children for whom you can volunteer to be a surrogate grandparent (or "aunt" or "uncle" if you are younger). Any of the ideas in this book can be adapted to surrogate grandparents.

One of the hardest days of all for children without grandparents is the annual Grandparents Day at school. While their classmates engage in special activities involving the grandparents, those children without often feel a painful awareness of their absence. Consider volunteering to serve as a surrogate grandparent on Grandparent's Day for a child you know.

Don't wait to be asked—volunteer! The need is there. The rewards are great, on earth and in heaven. There may be a match made in heaven waiting just for you!

OUR PRAYER

Dear heavenly Father,

You Yourself stretched out Your arms to the little children and invited them to come to You when you walked among them on earth. You taught us, "for of such is the Kingdom of Heaven." Open our eyes to see if there is any child or family to whom you desire that we stretch out our arms. Enlarge our hearts and grant us the desire to serve one another in love.

We ask this in the name of perfect love, our Lord Jesus,

Amen.

CONCLUSION

This is a message far bigger than the restoration of our families. It is a message of a loving God who longs to restore *His* family—His sons and His daughters—to Himself, family by family. He desires to be our Father, our Lord, and our Savior. Two thousand years ago, He sent His Son into this world to accomplish this magnificent mission. Now He is calling those who hear His voice to return to Him—and to lead their families back with them.

The restoration of our family relationships to the Lord is a call to us to separate from the world. Jesus declared that His kingdom is not of this world (John 18:3). Though He dwelt among men, He was not conformed to the patterns and practices of this world. *"For this world in its present form is passing away"* (1 Corinthians 7:31 NIV).

The biblical image of separating from the world is not a picture of fleeing or living in isolation from others. Quite to the contrary, it is a picture of living in fellowship with others, yet remaining unstained by and unconformed to the patterns and influences of this world. By remaining separate from the patterns of the world, our families can shine as lights in dark places. The time may be imminent when Christians will glorify God by serving as towers of light and beacons of courage to whom others will run for strength, comfort, and godly guidance.

All this is from God, who reconciled us to himself through Christ and gave us the ministry of reconciliation: that God was recon-

ciling the world to himself in Christ, not counting people's sins against them. And he has committed to us the message of reconciliation. We are therefore Christ's ambassadors, as though God were making his appeal through us. We implore you on Christ's behalf: Be reconciled to God (2 Corinthians 5:18–20).

If we can enter into eternity knowing that our children, and our grandchildren, and our great-grandchildren *love the Lord with all their hearts, with all their minds, and with all their strength,* then we have lived good and meaningful lives. May you, our dear readers, be blessed likewise.

EPILOGUE: THE CYCLE OF LIFE

It was Easter, and our family was gathered at our daughter and son-in-law's home to celebrate the resurrection of our Lord and Savior together. We ladies were busily preparing the meal when ten-year-old grandson Stephen meandered into the kitchen. At first, nothing struck me as unusual about a growing boy finding his way to the room with all the food.

"Are you looking for something to eat, Stephen?" I invited with a wink.

"No, Mom-Mom. I was just wondering what you were up to," Stephen replied in feigned innocence. "Hey, would you like to play with me?"

Never one to turn down an invitation to play with the grandchildren, I thought, *If this little guy wants to play, I'm ready!* Yet my intuition told me there was something suspicious about Stephen's demeanor. I could not help but notice that my girls were exchanging peculiar glances between them. I brushed off my suspicions and decided that entering spontaneously into a ten-year-old's world was more important at that moment. The girls could finish the meal prep without me.

"Sure, Stephen. I would love to play with you! What should we play?" I prompted him while drying my hands.

Unable to stifle her laughter a moment longer, Kim suddenly blurted out, "Mom, didn't you read Stephen's t-shirt?" With that, the girls burst into laughter, diffusing the tension in the kitchen.

Still bewildered, I read the words on Stephen's t-shirt slowly, "I–am–going–to–be–an–uncle."

"An UNCLE?? What?!!" I probed incredulously as the meaning began to sink in. That meant Roger and I were about to become GREAT-grandparents! Our granddaughter Julie was expecting her first baby!

How had the years passed so quickly? Our Kimberly was about to become a grandmother, while Robin and Lisa were to be great-aunts. While I did not *feel* old, I was awakened to the sober reality that the years had crept up on me. Roger and I thought we would be "pictures on the wall" by the time our grandchildren had children of their own. Being great-grandparents was uncharted territory for us—something we never dreamed we would experience. But God has had different plans for us.

Being great-grandparents was uncharted territory for us—something we never dreamed we would experience.

My thoughts quickly returned to the excitement in the kitchen. The girls had playfully sent Stephen into the living room to elicit Roger's reaction next. Having heard our exuberant outburst in the kitchen, Roger already suspected something fishy was in the air. It did not take him long to figure things out. Nudging Stephen playfully, Roger baited him in his typical, delightful, tongue-in-cheek manner, "So, Stephen, when are you going to be an uncle?" He knew ten-year-olds are completely clueless about matters of baby gestation.

"I dunno, Pop-Pop. I'm just the one wearing the t-shirt!"

It didn't take Roger long to seek me out in the kitchen. "Can you believe it, honey? GREAT-grandparents!" He chuckled in wonderment. The Lord was restoring what the locusts had eaten in Roger's family heritage—many times over!

Emotions were colliding inside my head and my heart. God had granted us the blessing of seeing *four* living generations. Joy and thankfulness for His goodness were right there on the surface, but so, too, was the question that had perplexed us decades earlier: "We're *great*-grandparents! NOW what do we do?" All I could think to blurt out to Roger was, "I'm afraid my poor brain is going to get all the generations mixed up!"

It was time for hugs all the way around. Then we enjoyed the happiest Easter dinner ever.

Six months later, on September 13, 2008, our first great-granddaughter, Mackenzie, came into this world. Julie was a mommy! Upon hearing the news, our first instinct was to immediately race to the hospital, just as we had done when our first grandchild was born. But suddenly, we caught ourselves, remembering that we were the *great*-grandparents now. *We* were not the grandparents. This was altogether different. We were being challenged to don yet another new hat in the cycle of life. Reluctantly, we accepted that it was now our season to step back and give Warren and Kim time alone with their daughter and son-in-law, bonding with their first grandchild.

Great-grandparenting is not stepping down into obscurity, but rather, it is a season of stepping back one more step in the ripples of life.

Roger and I arrived at the hospital, intentionally late in the afternoon, to find Julie looking radiant, just as her mother had looked the day she was born. Years of memories with Julie came flooding back. *She was so much like me—and so much like her mom, our daughter. Julie had grown into a strong, capable woman of faith. My thoughts meandered back to the time Julie offered me her diary to read, wanting to share with me her twelve-year-old feelings toward her brother, Jeff. At the time, Julie was upset with her brother, and she felt justified in "hating" him forever. She had wanted me to sympathize with her and affirm her side. Instead, I took the opportunity to draw her close with a story. As I listened to the things Julie was sharing, the window opened to talk about the seeds of bitterness that had taken root in her heart and her need to prune away those bitter roots so the bitter fruit would die. As was our custom, I ended by encouraging Julie to follow up by talking to her parents.*

"Mom-Mom? Would you like to hold your great-granddaughter?" Julie invited.

My thoughts snapped back to the present. *Would I ever!* It was a cherished moment. In my arms I was holding the first fruits of the *fourth generation* of the Roger R. Small family. The foundations of a godly legacy had been laid, and the mantle was being passed down through the generations—just as the Lord had promised.

Eight years have gone by, and we have been blessed with fifteen more great-grandchildren. And, Lord willing, more will be on the way! My fifth prayer journal for our family members is running out of pages; the knees of my pants have worn thin from prayer. Keeping up on photo albums has been too much for me, so pictures and memorabilia sit waiting in storage boxes.

Our final encouragement to all who read these pages is this: Great-grandparenting is not stepping down into obscurity, but rather, it is a season of stepping back one more step in the ripples of life. Roger and I are no longer in the center of the circle. It is now the season for our children to live out the role of grandparenting for themselves—and to learn to spread their wings and soar in the legacy that has been passed down to them. We admit that we felt a small twinge in our hearts the first time we were *not* invited to a family activity. That was new and unexpected for us. But our daughter quickly explained, "Mom and Dad, you taught us how to be grandparents by your own living example. We're grateful to you for that. Now *we* want to have this opportunity to follow in your footsteps." Roger and I were the ones who needed to prepare our hearts to assume a new role in a new season. Once again, *living* in this life began with *dying*. That is just the Lord's way. It is now our sons-in-law and daughters' turn to be grandparents. It is our season to step back.

My how the years have flown by! Roger's and my time on this side of eternity is winding down. Our eightieth birthdays are right around the corner. But this we know—grandparents *do* matter. We have an invaluable role to play in our extended family. The Bible declares that the sins of fathers are passed down to the third and fourth generations. However, through God's intervention with the atoning death and resurrection of His Son, the generational iniquities of a family can be completely turned around in one generation. Roger and I came to personal faith in the Lord Jesus Christ in 1970. Our conversions affected our whole family. My parents and Roger's father and stepmother shortly thereafter came to their own personal faith as they, too, surrendered their lives to the Lord. Even my Ginnah prayed to receive Jesus at the age of eighty! Truly the generations of the righteous are blessed. Jesus is our Righteousness. We owe Him nothing less than our lives. He is our blessing. And He is the most magnificent legacy we could ever leave to our children, and to our children's children, and beyond . . .

With Love from *Roger & Dottie*

Four Generations

GRANDMA'S HANDS

—© MELINDA CLEMENTS

Grandma, some ninety plus years, sat feebly on the patio bench. She didn't move, just sat with her head down staring at her hands.

When I sat down beside her she didn't acknowledge my presence and the longer I sat I wondered if she was OK.

Finally, not really wanting to disturb her but wanting to check on her at the same time, I asked her if she was OK. She raised her head and looked at me and smiled. "Yes, I'm fine, thank you for asking," she said in a clear voice strong.

"I didn't mean to disturb you, Grandma, but you were just sitting here staring at your hands and I wanted to make sure you were OK," I explained to her.

"Have you ever looked at your hands?" she asked. "I mean really looked at your hands?"

I slowly opened my hands and stared down at them. I turned them over, palms up and then palms down. No, I guess I had never really looked at my hands as I tried to figure out the point she was making.

Grandma smiled and related this story:

"Stop and think for a moment about the hands you have, how they have served you well throughout your years. These hands, though wrinkled shriveled and weak have been the tools I have used all my life to reach out and grab and embrace life.

They braced and caught my fall when as a toddler I crashed upon the floor.

They put food in my mouth and clothes on my back. As a child, my mother taught me to fold them in prayer. They tied my shoes and pulled on my boots. They held my husband and wiped my tears when he went off to serve our country in time of war.

They have been dirty, scraped and raw, swollen and bent. They were uneasy and clumsy when I tried to hold my newborn son. The left hand is decorated with my wedding band; they showed the world that I was married and loved someone special.

They wrote my letters to him and trembled and shook when I buried my parents and my spouse.

They have held my children and grandchildren, consoled neighbors, and shook in fists of anger when I didn't understand.

They have covered my face, combed my hair, and washed and cleansed the rest of my body. They have been sticky and wet, bent and broken, dried and raw. And to this day when not much of anything else of me works real well, but these hands hold me up, lay me down, and again continue to fold in prayer.

These hands are the mark of where I've been and the ruggedness of life.

But more importantly it will be these hands that God will reach out and take when He leads me home. And with my hands He will lift me to His side and there I will use these hands to touch His Face."

I will never look at my hands the same again. But I remember God reached out and took my Grandma's hands and led her home.

When my hands are hurt or sore or when I stroke the face of my children and husband I think of Grandma. I know she has been stroked and caressed and held by the Hands of God.

ACKNOWLEDGEMENTS

TO KAREN DAVIS:

We would like to express our gratitude to our Lord for sending Karen into our lives. This would not be a book without her gifting. Karen has spent hours and hours writing and rewriting the information we shared with her. It has taken two years to complete. Karen has patiently waited before the Lord for the right words to express our hearts and to make our message clear to the reader. Thank you, Karen, for your faithfulness to write God's words. May your words be a blessing to many, as the Lord restores His family. We love you, sister.

TO MARLENE BAGNULL:

We want to thank Marlene for her words of encouragement to keep going. She was a great inspiration to us to learn ways to improve our writing. The Lord has had His way in the writing of this book, in un-expected "re-routes," and we are grateful to Marlene for her valuable directions along the way.

TO MARILYN DAILEY:

We are so grateful to Marilyn for the time she volunteered to read this book. Her grandmother's eyes have been of great importance, and her "grammar glasses" have been spotless! We appreciate Marilyn's kindness in the midst of family activities and traveling. She has been a faithful friend to us over the years.

EDITOR'S NOTE

PROGRESSIVE VERSUS PRISTINE:
GOD'S CALL TO RESTORE FAMILIES

As a writer, I love words. I love the way an apt word can impart the perfect flavor to a passage. As the Author of our faith, the Lord Himself places supreme value on words. From infinity past, God has chosen to reveal Himself as the pre-eminent, eternal *Word*. *"In the beginning was the **Word**, and the **Word** was with God, and the **Word** was God"* (John 1:1, emphasis mine). When the Lord descended from His throne in heaven to dwell among us, He came as the *living* Word, revealed in the person of Jesus Christ. There is something glorious about God's words! They are His power in creation and salvation!

Neither the Lord nor human writers choose words randomly. Rather, words are chosen intentionally, both for their literal meanings and their implied meanings. If I were to attempt the challenging but futile assignment of choosing *one* word from our limited human vocabulary that depicts God's perfect plan for His creation, I might be inclined to settle on the word *pristine*. With curiosity piqued, I cracked open a dictionary for the exact definition of *pristine*, believing it held the key to understanding God's plan for restoring and strengthening families, and ultimately His church in our time.

pristine: [pris'-teen, pri-steen'] adjective: in its original condition; pure; an unblemished state.

To refer to something as *pristine* implies that it is in its *original, unspoiled condition.* A pristine lake, for example, is a clear, pure, unpolluted lake.

In contrast to the denotation of pristine, *progress* is defined as movement *away from* the original state. Progress is presumed to be movement toward an *improved* state or a *higher* goal—one that is considered superior to the original condition. To give an example, some might consider it progress to replace rural countryside with high-rise buildings or shopping malls. Progress, however, is not always an improvement over the original design. The most beautiful hue of new paint brushed over a cracked, marred surface still reveals the brokenness that lies beneath the surface. Often, something that has deteriorated must first be restored to its *pristine* condition before *progress* can truly be considered an improvement. It's a two-step process: take off the old, put on the new.

Yet God's blueprint for families... has fallen victim to the timeless conflict between progressive currents and pristine foundations.

Consider a second analogy: the foundation of a building that has been weakened by cracks or fractures. Any competent engineer would most certainly not design improvements over a flawed foundation. In the name of structural integrity, the engineer would repair the foundation first, restoring it to its pristine condition. Under the pretense of *progress*, one can make many lavish upgrades, but unless the foundation has first been restored to a strong, unblemished state, the building it supports stands at risk of collapsing.

So what does all this have to do with God's plan for restoring and strengthening families?

Going back in time, to a time when the foundations of humanity were laid, we read in Scripture that God's original design for families was a pristine design. His creation was pure, unblemished by sin. In the garden of Eden, God created a man and a woman, putting them together as a family and declaring His creation good. Then sin entered in.

Today, we are living in what have been dubbed *progressive* times. And we are induced to believe that is a good thing. Yet God's blueprint for families—the very foundation of our culture and of His church—has fallen victim to the timeless conflict between progressive currents and pristine foundations. Changes in God's original design for families are occurring at lightning speed. In the name of progressive adaptation to the current of our times, even the basic definition of *family* is being altered. Consequently, the composition of family units has been radically changed from God's original, pristine plan—the plan that He declared *good*.

Unless we rebuild families according to the Lord's design, we will be vulnerable to destruction.

Perhaps no one would say that his or her *intended* outcome has been to weaken families, yet that has been the inevitable result. Destructive forces are fracturing the very foundations of families.

Powers and principalities in the heavenly realm are at war. On earth, the desire to align oneself with the progressive thinkers of our day battles against the good and perfect will of our Father in heaven. Many families today are losing the battle, becoming like tarnished—yet still valuable—treasures, needing desperately to be restored, so their strength, beauty, and value can shine forth and impact the world around them.

What will happen when the winds of trials or the onslaught of tribulations begin to blow against progressive family structures that have been built upon weak foundations? Unless we rebuild families according to the Lord's design, we will be vulnerable to destruction.

Now is the time to drop a plumb line from heaven—the plumb line of God's Word—and use it as our guide to restore strong families. If the foundation is strong, families will be prepared to withstand the assaults of our times. And if individual families are strong, our society, our nation, and our churches will be better equipped to stand firm, as lights to the nations. God's design for families is not only a pristine plan, but it is also the *perfect* plan.

There *is* hope. Though battles may have been lost, the war can yet be won. In these treacherous, changing times, we believe God has a plan to restore and equip extended families to stand strong against assaults. *We believe grandparents interrelating across the generations play a fundamental role in God's plan to strengthen families.* While God's plan begins with the restoration of families, ultimately, His plan extends to the restoration of His kingdom on earth!

The impact you make increases exponentially with each successive generation.

Our hope is that we will come to value God's pristine designs more than the progress of mankind. Our hope is that Jesus will once again be lifted up as Lord, to the glory of His Father. That is our urgent hope for the restoration of our nation. We want it to be the legacy we leave to our heirs as well. Our coveted reward will be the favor and blessings of God upon our families and upon our nation.

Perhaps you are thinking, "But what can *I* do to make a difference? I'm just one grandparent in one family. How much difference can I really make?" The reality is, you *can* make a difference. You can influence your children and your grandchildren, who in turn will influence *their* grandchildren, and each generation will, in turn, influence *their* spheres of relationships. As the ripples continue multiplying, so does your influence. The impact you make increases exponentially with each successive generation. You will never know the full impact of your life during your lifetime, but you can rest assured that you play an important role in God's much bigger plan!

The fitting and God-honoring response for us today is to return humbly and gratefully to the wonderful Designer of families. Though we may never attain an unblemished state on this side of eternity, let us not lose sight of the higher goal of the upward call of God in Christ Jesus. We *can* repent and seek the Lord for restoration of our families and our nation.

> *If My people who are called by My name will humble themselves, and pray and seek My face, and turn from their wicked ways, then I will hear from heaven, and will forgive their sin and heal their land* (2 Chronicles 7:14).

When I first began to join Roger and Dottie in prayer over their vision for this book, the idea that *grandparents* might play a very real and significant role in the greater scheme of God's plan was a new idea for me. But as I started searching the Scriptures, what has become increasingly evident is the vital role that God intends for older generations to play in the lives of the generations that follow.

As a longtime friend of the Smalls, I have had the privilege of a front-row view of their lives and their family dynamics. I can attest to the amazing legacy of love and wisdom this couple has passed down to their family—and to the good fruit it has borne. Roger and Dottie's lives validate the truths they have written in this book!

—K.B.D.

ABOUT THE AUTHORS

After growing up in New England, Roger and Dottie Small have lived most of their fifty-year marriage in the greater Philadelphia area. Roger, with degrees in engineering and business, provided for his family as an industrial salesman. Far from being ready to retire at 80 years old, Roger is currently pursuing another master's degree while working as a financial advisor. An entertaining storyteller, Roger spins stories on the spot (undoubtedly all true!) for any occasion!

Dottie has had the privilege of fulfilling her calling as a helpmate to her husband and as a stay-at-home mom (and grandmom!). She has served her local church tirelessly and is much sought after for her wisdom and godly counsel. Her contagious joy and fitting encouragements are an inspiration to all who know her.

Together, this vivacious couple takes great delight in their three married daughters and sons-in-law, thirteen grandchildren, and sixteen great-grandchildren—with two more on the way! It is their desire to remain active in ministry in their home church, while continuing to encourage and support families, both young and "older"! Visit the blog *Thoughts to Ponder* at dottieinhim.blogspot.com for more insights from Dottie.